WHAT'S YOUR ANGER TYPE?

♦♦♦

PETER ANDREW SACCO Ph.D.

Copyright © 2006 Peter Andrew Sacco Ph.D.

10-Digit ISBN 1-59113-908-2
13-Digit ISBN 978-1-59113-908-9

All rights reserved. No part of this publication may be reproduced, stored in a retrieval system, or transmitted in any form or by any means, electronic, mechanical, recording or otherwise, without the prior written permission of the author.

Printed in the United States of America.

Booklocker.com, Inc.
2006

Cover design by New Perspectives
Copyright 2006

DISCLAIMER

The author and publisher are providing this book and its contents on an "as is" basis and make no representations or warranties of any kind with respect to this book or its contents. The author and publisher disclaim all such representations and warranties, including for example warranties of merchantability and fitness for a particular purpose. In addition, the author and publisher do not represent or warrant that the information accessible via this book is accurate, complete or current.

The statements made about products and services have not been evaluated by the U.S. Food and Drug Administration. They are not intended to diagnose, treat, cure, or prevent any condition or disease. Please consult with your own physician or healthcare specialist regarding the suggestions and recommendations made in this book.

Except as specifically stated in this book, neither the author or publisher, nor any authors, contributors, or other representatives will be liable for damages arising out of or in connection with the use of this book. This is a comprehensive limitation of liability that applies to all damages of any kind, including (without limitation) compensatory; direct, indirect or consequential damages; loss of data, income or profit; loss of or damage to property and claims of third parties.

You understand that this book is not intended as a substitute for consultation with a licensed healthcare practitioner, such as your physician. Before you begin any physical or mental healthcare program, or change your lifestyle in any way, you will consult your physician or other licensed healthcare practitioner to ensure that you are in good health and that the examples contained in this book will not harm you. This book provides content related to topics about anger management. As such, use of this book implies your acceptance of this disclaimer.

At the time of this printing, the author and several colleagues were in production for the video supplement *"What's Your Anger Type?"*

To learn more about this book, other books written by the author, or the video please visit www.petersacco.com or www.vicesmagazine.com.

FORWARD

"What Is Your Anger Type?" is a very informative, enlightening, educational and entertaining book which sheds tremendous light on the whole emotion of anger! I strongly recommend this book for anyone dealing with their own personal anger management issues, or living with those possessing anger management problems.

I am an individual who has dealt with her own fair share of anger issues which were a bi-product of my addiction/use and recovery. The concepts and strategies in this book helped me not only with my anger management and aggression issues, but also with my recovery for substance abuse. It helped me understand why I was angry, why I carried a chip on both shoulders and then to come up with ways for creating positive change in my life.

Whether you are young or old, male or female, Western or Eastern culture, this book will definitely help you if you apply the principles Peter teaches. If you are a parent or a teacher, I would highly recommend this book if you have a short fuse around children. I know my anger types, now I hope you find yours and do something positive! Good luck!

ANDREA P.
TORONTO, CA

ACKNOWLEDGEMENTS

What Is Your Anger Type was created because of the countless individuals; clients, students and colleagues who believe I have the insights to help those with anger management problems. This book was made possible from the experiences, successes, failures and ideas those I have been involved with have shared with me. Huge thanks to all of you.

I am very thankful to the many universities, colleges, institutions, agencies and television programs who have invited me in the past, present and future to speak to their large audiences. I would also like to thank the professionals who also specialize in anger management for being pioneers in the field and continued innovators.

I would also like to thank the friends and staff involved with Vices Magazine. They continually encourage me to keep writing and educating. Through Vices magazine, I am very grateful to have had the chance to speak with or meet such great roles models as; Jack Canfield, Dr. Robert Schuller, Dr. Bernie Seigel, Mark Victor Hansen, Dr. William Glasser, Dr. Susan Weitzman and countless others who added great insights which I was able to incorporate into What's Your Anger Type. A special thanks to Jen Schott and Dr. Abraham!

PETER ANDREW SACCO Ph.D.

For all of you who read this book, I hope it helps you with whatever struggles you are having with your emotions. Always remember one thing, you can feel and think whatever you choose. You don't have to be angry!

♎

CONTENTS

1 AN INFORMAL INTRODUCTION TO YOUR ANGER......... 1
2 AND YOUR ANGER TYPE IS?...................................... 13
3 RESISTANT & PASSIVE ANGER 33
4 INTERNET & COMPUTER RAGE 47
5 ADDICTIVE ANGER 55
6 PETRIFIED ANGER 65
7 COMPRESSIVE ANGER 79
8 JEALOUSY 91
9 ROAD RAGE 103
10 CONFLICTUAL ANGER 117
11 HABITUAL ANGER 127
12 PASSIVE-AGGRESSION 137
13 MORALISTIC ANGER 149
14 MANIPULATIVE ANGER 161
15 WHAT MOTIVATES YOUR   ANGER?.................... 175
16 ANGRY PERSONALITIES 189
17 HOW TO MANAGE YOUR ANGER! 223
18 CHILDREN AND ANGER 263
19 TIRED OF FIGHTING? 273

APPENDICES 281
   REFERENCE SOURCES 283
   RECOMMENDED READINGS...289
ABOUT PETER ANDREW SACCO..293

1

AN INFORMAL INTRODUCTION TO YOUR ANGER…

☠

In the beginning the universe was created. This has made a lot of people angry and been widely regarded as a bad move.

Douglas Adams

WHAT'S YOUR ANGER TYPE?

Do you have an anger management problem? Is there something or someone around you, or in your life who is always getting under your skin? Do you just want to explode? Do you feel like you are literally at the end of your "anger control leash"? If you answered yes to any of these questions, then this book can definitely help you and perhaps even save you from detrimental situations!

Let's face it... everyone gets angry. Anger is a normal and acceptable human emotion just as happiness, joy, surprise, sadness and angst. Unfortunately, most times anger is expressed in non-productive and unacceptable ways which society deems as inappropriate. No one complains about individuals who are happy all the time. Well, some people might actually start wondering about you if are always smiling. That is definitely a good thing! Similarly, most wouldn't be insensitive to individuals who are experiencing bouts of sadness. Why then is anger looked at in a less productive light? Perhaps it is due to the few isolated incidents which make news and media because someone has behaved so badly when they were enraged. Maybe, it could be due to the urban legends/myths of people becoming "superhuman" monsters during their fits of rage leading them to kill! Could it be how movies and television portray anger and vengeance for wrong doings? How far will people go when they are angry? Could they really lose it mentally, psychology and emotionally when they become enraged? Have you ever experienced meltdown?

Interestingly, everyone has the ability to control all facets of how they act, due to how they feel, which in turn is precipitated by their thought processes. We can all control our anger because we can all control the seeds which start the process... our thoughts!

Think angry thoughts → *Feel angry* → *Act angry* → *Become angry*

This is the flowchart process I use when working with clients to explain how and why they become angry. I will definitely explain it in greater detail later in the book. I want you to examine briefly in order to see my personal stance on how I believe anger begins, flourishes and ends. Stay tuned!

Anyone reading this book will learn the following 8 key points:

1) If we think it, we'll feel it, we'll act that way, and over a long period of time, we may even take on that behavior and

become it... an angry person.

2) Anger is a normal and healthy emotion. All people emote and if we all emote, we are capable of becoming angry at any point in our lives.

3) Since we are all able to exert control over our emotions, then we can determine how we choose to express our anger.

4) Anger is a secondary emotion. Some other emotion or thought process always comes before anger.

5) There are 12 different types of anger and most of us possess some, even many of them given different situations and periods in our lives.

6) We all possess a distinct behavioral style for dealing with the world and people around us.

7) There are ways for managing and controlling your anger in more effective and productive ways if you are willing

to work at it.

8) Its never too late to modify negative, destructive expressions of anger and replace them with optimal, acceptable alternatives.

9) The same simple rules for managing anger apply to everyone, equally to both males and females and even children.

10) Its okay to laugh at yourself sometime. Hey, I am sure others do!

👍

IN A SENTENCE OR TWO WHAT BOTHERS YOU THE MOST?

Before delving any further into this book, take a few minutes, or longer if you require to take a casual self-inventory of your own anger. Moreover, pay close attention to all the specific people, places, situations and things which contribute to your anger. List anything and everything you can think of no

WHAT'S YOUR ANGER TYPE?

matter how foolish or absurd things may sound.

Things that I get angry most at are...

1.

2.

3.

4.

5.

6.

7.

8.

9.

10.

* Hopefully, you haven't had to count past 10! If so, don't fret.

Now that you have listed your top 10 anger precipitators, compare them with the most common irritants people usually report as being their all-time triggers. As you look through the list, see if you can pick out a common theme.

COMMON ANGER TRIGGERS

1. spouse
2. children
3. co-workers
4. boss
5. traffic
6. rude people
7. dogs pooping on your lawn
8. bad weather (too much rain/snow)
9. governments/politicians
10. taxes

11. long line-ups
12. bad drivers
13. inflation
14. drunk people
15. gossipers
16. slow restaurant service
17. congested parking lots
18. messy kids/spouses
19. people who cheat
20. sports teams you root for who always lose
21. bad parents
22. rules which make no sense
23. racism/discrimination
24. TV/cable problems
25. bad Internet service
26. people who talk during movies
27. obnoxious sports fans
28. people who let you down
29. plans which fall through/disappointment
30. people who abuse the social assistance/support system
31. tardiness in others
32. self

33. when life treats you unfairly
34. stupidity
35. barking dogs
36. babies crying uncontrollably
37. hard to follow directions/instructions
38. people who smoke in your space
39. ban on smoking (for smokers)
40. people who stand too close or sit too close to you and invade your personal space
41. when someone wakes you up
42. telemarketers
43. door to door solicitors
44. when someone doesn't listen to you or understand you
45. litter bugs
46. people who don't flush toilets/urinals
47. road construction
48. trains holding up traffic
49. plane delays
50. things/cars breaking down

How many "irritants" on the list were you able to relate too as "triggers" for your own anger? Throughout this book I

WHAT'S YOUR ANGER TYPE?

will use these two terms "irritants" and "triggers" to refer to those people, events or things you attribute to causing you to experience anger. Also, I will show you how nothing can make you angry unless you allow it that power. Even though something from the above list can attribute to your anger, it can't make you angry! Nothing can make you angry on it's own unless you let it! When you look at the title of this book *What's Your Anger Type?*, you're probably asking yourself is there more than one type of anger, and if so what type(s) of anger do I have? Identifying what type of anger you possess is probably the best place to start. Once you identify your anger type, then you can identify your triggers/irritants and modify behaviors, situations and perceptions to create new ways of feeling.

2

AND YOUR ANGER TYPE IS?

☹

The biggest misconception about me is that I'm angry and violent. But I'm a real sweetie.
                                                Jack Nicholson

WANT TO KNOW WHAT YOUR ANGER TYPE IS?

If you want to know more about what type of anger you possess, it would be a good idea to complete the self-administered questionnaire. The outcome of the questionnaire will show you what types of anger exist and which one(s) you possess. In subsequent chapters, you will be provided with explanations and descriptions of each anger type. The questions I have created have been developed from administering hundreds of sample questions to hundreds of clients, patients, students, employee assistant program participants and general interest groups who have shown common characteristics for patterns of anger. I have selected 36 of the best possible questions which illuminate specific anger types. Please take a few moments to complete the following questionnaire following the specified directions.

WHAT'S YOUR ANGER TYPE QUIZ

You will need a pen or pencil to complete this test. On a separate sheet of paper please make a list from 1-36 or circle your answers in the book. For each question, write down the corresponding score which best describes your feeling. When completing this quiz, it is very important to think about your answers in the present moment. Do not answer questions based on how you once behaved or how you wish you behaved. The best way to determine your particular anger type (s) is to be as honest as possible and give yourself the rating which first comes to mind. Do not rationalize or think too much about each question. Also, do not get worried if you feel you are answering too many questions as being "most of the time". Just because you answer a lot of questions as being true of your feelings and behaviors does not make you crazy, sick or insane! The purpose of this quiz is not to diagnose, but rather to identify anger patterns and types to make appropriate thought, feeling and behavior modifications.

Please give yourself a numerical score for each question. Write down the number which best represents how you are feeling, thinking or behaving in that particular situation.

0 - Does Not Pertain To Me
1 - Sometimes True For Me
3 - Often The Case For Me

WHAT'S YOUR ANGER TYPE?

5 - Always The Case For Me

1. No matter what the situation is, I try to never get mad. To get mad would not be good.

    0   (1)   3   5

2. Whenever my computer screen freezes up I impatiently pound on the mouse. I don't have time for this crap!

    0   (1)   3   5

3. I like getting angry because it really pumps me up. I feel like I can do anything when I am angry.

    (0)   1   3   5

4. When I get angry I stay angry for a long time. It's just so hard to let it go.

0   (1)   3   5

5. I tend to really lose emotional control when I get mad. I just can't think rationally.

0   (1)   3   5

6. In my relationships I tend to get jealous quite easily.

0   (1)   3   5

7. I tend to get really annoyed whenever I get stuck in traffic jams. I have no patience.

0   (1)   3   5

WHAT'S YOUR ANGER TYPE?

8. I find myself easily getting into arguments and debates with others over trivial things.

    0   (1)   3   5

9. There is rarely a day that goes by in which I don't get mad.

    (0)   1   3   5

10. When I am angry I usually like to hide my feelings and pretend I am not angry.

    (0)   1   3   5

11. I really get upset whenever someone puts me down or insults me.

    0   (1)   3   5

12. I am most motivated whenever I am angry. My anger moves me toward action.

    0   (1)   3   5

13. I feel very uncomfortable whenever I am faced with confrontations or conflicts. I try to avoid them.

    0   1   (3)   5

14. I get so angry when I get pop ups on my Internet. I curse and swear. Damn advertisements!

    (0)   1   3   5

15. Watching fights in sports, on television or in real life excites me. I actually get pumped up!

    (0)   1   3   5

WHAT'S YOUR ANGER TYPE?

16. Forgiving others who have wronged me is very difficult. I just can't seem to forgive and forget.

(0)   1   3   5

17. The best way to describe me when I am mad is a time bomb. I get so angry I explode!

0   (1)   3   5

18. I tend to have a habit of putting people down behind their backs.

0   (1)   3   5

19. Whenever someone cuts me off when I am driving, I curse them with fingers or fist gestures and yell at them.

(0)   1   3   5

20. I like to prepare for an argument with someone even though they have no idea it is coming. I argue to win!

(0)   1   3   5

21. I am angry most of the time throughout the course of a day. This seems to be a common feeling I experience.

(0)   1   3   5

22. I don't get mad... I prefer to get even!

0   (1)   3   5

23. Whenever I discuss my personal beliefs or ideals, I find myself defending them aggressively. If people don't like what I think or believe, then to heck with them!

(0)   1   3   5

WHAT'S YOUR ANGER TYPE?

24. I find when I am angry I can get what I want much easier. My anger gets me what I want!

(0)   1   3   5

25. I have always been taught anger is bad and I should never show it.

0   (1)   3   5

26. Nothing annoys me more than telemarketers... they piss me off! What gives them the right to call my house?

0   (1)   3   5

27. Whenever I get angry or someone around me does, I get really excited. My heart starts to race and I feel things getting out of control.

    0   (1)   3   5

28. I tend to relive the wrongs people have done to me over and over in my head. I just can't shake these thoughts!

    0   (1)   3   5

29. When I get angry I punch, throw or break things.

    (0)   1   3   5

30. I dislike people who get everything they want in life. Why does everyone else get the breaks?

    (0)   1   3   5

WHAT'S YOUR ANGER TYPE?

31. When people in front of me drive too slow, I get angry. They shouldn't be driving if they don't drive the speed limit!

    0   **(1)**   3   5

32. I tend to find fault with people and things in life. I just wish things would be more the way I would like them to be.

    (0)   1   3   5

33. I have dreams in which I get into fights and come out the winner. I like these kinds of dreams because they make me feel good even though they are not real.

    (0)   1   3   5

34. If someone has hurt me or wronged me, I will see to it they experience the same kind of hurt as well.

(0)   1   3   5

35. I can't talk about politics, religion or personal subjects without feeling myself getting upset or even angry. These types of topics should not be discussed as they only lead to disagreements.

(0)   1   3   5

36. I tend to work best under stress and pressure. I prefer deadlines because I seem to always get things done at the last minute.

0   (1)   3   5

WHAT'S YOUR ANGER TYPE?

Please tally your score (the numbers you circled). Once you have tabulated your score, compare them with the following measures:

150 - 180 points   *Severe Anger Problems*

120 - 149 points   *Moderate Anger Problems*

80 - 119 points   *Mild Anger Management Problems*

30 - 79 points   *Stressed/Frustrated Easily*

0 - 29 points   *Cool As A Cucumber*

👍

Just because you had a score which was extremely high (the severe anger management domain) don't fret. I will provide you with tools for dealing with your anger problems later in the book. For now though, it's not your total score you'll focus on, rather the subset scores which match up to each specific category of anger.

PETER ANDREW SACCO Ph.D.

There are 12 types of anger you were tested for. Your anger usually falls within one of the these 12 anger types. In order to better understand which specific type of anger you possess, please re-tally your scores using the following method.

Add your scores in threes combining the questions in the following groups:

Subgroups

1	*Questions: 1, 13, 25*
2	*Questions: 2, 14, 26*
3	*Questions: 3, 15, 27*
4	*Questions: 4, 16, 28*
5	*Questions: 5, 17, 29*
6	*Questions: 6, 18, 30*
7	*Questions: 7, 19, 31*
8	*Questions: 8, 20, 32*
9	*Questions: 9, 21, 33*
10	*Questions: 10, 22, 34*
11	*Questions: 11, 23, 35*
12	*Questions: 12, 24, 36*

WHAT'S YOUR ANGER TYPE?

For each subgroup, you will have a different score. Each score will represent a specific type of anger. Once you have a score for each subgroup, please compare the score with the matching measures:

MEASURES		
	12 - 15	*Very High*
	9 - 11	*High*
	5 - 8	*Moderate*
	1 - 4	*Low*

If you scored in the *"Very High"* or *"High"* range for the 3 questions in each subgroup, then you possess the characteristics for that specific type of anger. Generally, most people score high or very high in a couple of the specific categories for anger. Keep in mind, the type of anger you possess may change or shift depending on what events are taking place in your life. Also, since most of us experience stress and frustration as a by-product of the busy lives we lead, it would be expected to possess some type of anger some of the time. Really, when you think about it, no one is immune to anger!

Each of the subtypes of anger possesses an "anger component" at the core of the domain, however how the anger evolved and why it continues to transgress occurs for different reasons. In the subsequent chapters, you will be provided with a working definition for each type of anger focusing on it's beginnings, it's M.O. (method of operation) and it's typical outcome.

The following subgroups of questions matched up with each distinguished anger type:

SUBGROUP	ANGER TYPE
1	*Resistant/Passive*
2	*Internet/Computer Rage*
3	*Addictive Anger*
4	*Petrified Anger*
5	*Compressive Anger*

WHAT'S YOUR ANGER TYPE?

6 *Jealousy*

7 *Road Rage*

8 *Conflictual Anger*

9 *Habituated Anger*

10 *Passive-Aggression*

11 *Moralistic Anger*

12 *Manipulative Anger*

3

RESISTANT & PASSIVE ANGER

❖

If you kick a stone in anger, you'll hurt your own foot.

Korean Proverb

WHAT'S YOUR ANGER TYPE?

When you were a child, did your parents ever tell you anger is "bad" and you should never show it? Were you ever punished for getting upset and then banished to your bedroom, or if in school, to the corner? Perhaps your parents were of the mindset "children should be seen and not heard"? If you scored "high" or "very high" for the questions pertaining to resistant/passive anger, then you may have issues with anger as an emotion!

Resistant/passive anger is the type of anger learned from parents, role models and teachers who lack emotional expression or dismiss anger as a healthy emotion. In fact, this type of anger is passed on from generation to generation by those who are adverse to expressing emotions they view as negative. They also try to avoid all forms of conflict in their lives. They endorse an affirmation that "anger is bad" and should be avoided at all times. Some families and cultures view the expression of anger as a weakness! They believe when one expresses emotions such as anger and sadness, they are revealing their psychological weaknesses. Moreover, media (TV shows and movies) usually portray angry people as really "losing it". Some movies have gone so far in depicting anger as a mental health illness requiring committal to a psychiatric ward or serious on-going counseling. Is it any wonder some people avoid anger like the plague?

When you were a child growing up, were you around parents and family members who argued and fought all the time? Did the constant fighting give you butterflies and make your stomach upset? Did you worry someone was going to get hurt? Perhaps it was you? Another of the reasons resistant/passive anger effects people is from being raised in dysfunctional families where fighting often occurred. Most times, things ended badly, where conflicts were not resolved. Family members literally let the sun go down with anger weighing heavy in their hearts. You might have felt so sad and helpless from the bickering and fighting that you just withdrew. You may have felt totally helpless and made a conscious promise to never get angry or disagree with anyone because it might lead to similar fighting. The groundwork was laid and you literally trained the mind to avoid anger at all costs by keeping everything inside. This is not good! Did you know that anger turned inward and never expressed sometimes has the ability to take on a detrimental emotion called depression?

If you keep everything inside of yourself and never vent your frustrations, anger and emotions, these feelings are going to rot inside of you like some old cheese you leave in the back of the refrigerator. In the beginning you know what anger is. The more you keep suppressing it you lose track of what it is exactly. It literally becomes some kind of disfigured entity like moldy cheese which becomes discolored and hard to discern anymore. The longer it stays in the tray and bacteria cultures, it becomes more difficult to clean. Often time people suffering from depression will colorfully describe their moods as gray or black all the time. That is what depression feels like for many... a dark pit! They feel helpless, hopeless and hapless. They feel they have little or no control over their lives. They feel like their opinions don't matter and no one cares. Why is that? For starters, they don't dare speak up because they might offend, challenge, or better still... make someone angry! According to this type of anger, you must avoid anger at all costs even if that means making yourself feel ill.

Here are some situations where resistant anger is at its worst. Can you see yourself in any of these situations?

Scenario #1

Sandra is fed up with people using her. She feels like she is always giving to people but never getting anything in return. One of her closest friends Amanda is the prime culprit in her books. She feels Amanda takes advantage of her and uses her. She has a hard time saying "no" to Amanda's requests. She worries however if she refuses her, Amanda might like her less or not want to be her friend at all! This really bothers Sandra. She has made a conscious decision to say "no" next time Amanda asks her to baby sit her kids. A friend from Sandra's past calls her and invites her to go to a concert this coming Friday night. Sandra is ecstatic and can't wait to go. The next day Amanda calls her and asks her to baby sit the same night as the concert. Amanda tells her it is so important as she has the "dream date" of her life. Sandra can hear the loud "no's" screaming in her head. Before she even knows what happened, she has agreed to baby sit Amanda's kids thus forfeiting going to the Friday concert. She is so upset with Amanda. She hates Amanda! She hates herself for agreeing!

What is the cause of Sandra's anger? Her inability to say no due to her fear of rejection.

What are the precipitating factors? Others know they can take advantage of Sandra so they place burdens and decisions on her they know they can get away with. Sandra is a pleaser due to her low self-esteem as she worries if she becomes her own person people will stop liking her. Do these friends of hers actually like and respect her?

Scenario #2

Ivan asks Nick if he wants to see a movie Saturday night. Nick's response is, "yeah, if you want too." Ivan asks Nick which movie he would like to see. "I don't know, whatever you want," replies Nick. "Do you want me to pick you up or do you want to get me?" Ivan asks Nick. Nick shrugs his shoulders, "Doesn't matter to me." Ivan asks Nick if he prefers to see the early show or the late show. "Either one is okay with me," replies Nick. Ivan starts to feel very frustrated with Nick's indecisiveness. Nick on the other hand, feels very pressured by Ivan asking him to make choices. Ivan wishes he would have never asked Nick to hang out with him in the first place.

What is the cause of Nick's resistant anger? He doesn't know how to make decisions for himself. He tends to go with the flow, never being the initiator.

What are the precipitating factors? Nick has probably had people plan things for him in the past and help make his decisions for him. It is a good bet Nick has never been taught how to be assertive. In fact, he has probably been coddled by over-protective parents. Ivan on the other hand becomes frustrated and annoyed over Nick's indecisiveness. Nick perceives Ivan's invite as a burden to him forcing him to invest mental effort in making a decision.

Scenario #3

Kelly was taught by her parents at an early age little girls should be seen and not heard. As a 25 year old lady, she now works for a firm as a secretarial assistant. She feels her boss and other co-workers place unrealistic workloads on her desk. She is unable to get caught up. Her boss has asked her on occasion if she would like an assistant to help her. She has blatantly refused to have an assistant stating everything is under control. The stress from work is really getting to her. She rarely sleeps, eats and is miserable most of the time. She has grown to hate going to work. She resents her boss more each day. Noticing her recent discomfort and unhappiness, her boss requests a meeting with her to discuss her mood swings. She assures her boss everything is fine and that it's a woman thing, not to worry. He suggests bringing in an assistant and she argues she doesn't need one. In fact, she requests more work to take home for the weekend as she claims this is her passion. Her boss gives in to her requests. Weeks later, while leaving work late one afternoon, she notices she has left her keys inside the car and the doors are locked. Kelly picks a large chunk of brick and starts bashing in the driver's window before smashing all the windows. She cowers to the ground and begins to break down.

What is the cause of Kelly's anger? Being stressed and overworked.

What are the precipitating factors? Kelly's main problem is she doesn't know how to do things in moderation. She doesn't seek help when she needs it and when it is offered to her. She has learned to keep everything inside and not be a burden to others. Most important, Kelly does not have an outlet for her stress. She needs to learn to get the emotional garbage out before it *festers inside of her, thus leading to her emotional breakdown.*

Have you ever heard the term *"nervous breakdown"*? Clinically speaking, there is no such thing. Perhaps the best way to refer to this loosely slung, slang term is to view it as mental burnout. The precipitating cause is persistent or escalating stress in one's life which leads to unceasing frustration. Eventually, you get to the point where you can't take it anymore and reach meltdown. Here are some of the signs and symptoms to look for with this type of anger:

- chronic fatigue
- nausea/vomiting
- constant colds
- small aches/pains
- feeling tired and run down
- loss of appetite
- sleep disturbances/insomnia
- mental flashbacks
- frequent crying spells
- suicidal thoughts
- social isolation/withdrawing

- drinking/drug use
- pessimism
- irrational fears
- depression

Interestingly, depression seems to be the most common by-product of resistant anger. The individual is so pre-occupied with not being angry that they become highly focused on the emotion unconsciously. Consequently, what happens is the anger is turned inward and manifests itself in the form of depression. Rather than expel the negative feelings which are building inside you, you hold onto them and try to extinguish them inside of yourself. Sure the anger gets watered down, however it becomes diluted into a more "acceptable" emotion for yourself... depression.

Think about it for a moment. What emotion is more likely to receive greater empathy and sympathy? Anger or depression? If you're angry, people avoid you because they perceive you as dangerous. On the other hand, if you are depressed, you are perceived to be less of a threat. In fact, people will actually start to feel sorry for you and actually enable your depression. So you actually get to be "accepted" more readily for being depressed.

Have you ever been around someone or know someone who constantly complains all the time? Are they always complaining about some ache or pain? They are never happy! Do you literally have to pull teeth whenever you try to get them to make a decision or commit to something? Well, this resistant type of anger allows this person to engage in this passive, helpless mindset where they rely on others to make their decisions for them. Some individuals with resistant anger could be classified as possessing an almost "sadomasochistic" nature. In fact, the only time they feel alive is when they are "in pain" or complaining about something. From my work with clients, these are some of the behavioral attributes individuals with this anger type display:

- allowing others to make decisions for them
- feeling used and unappreciated
- frustrating to others because they show no initiative or assertion
- saying yes when they want to say no
- being in situations they don't want to be in
- blaming others for their unhappiness

- constantly seeking other's approval
- feeling like every situation is the same

The bottom line with this anger type is they never feel good about themselves. The world is always unfair to them. They were dealt a bad hand of cards. There is some sort of conspiracy going on where everyone is against them. They just don't understand why things are the way things are. They have developed a method of self-defeating thinking and they have trapped themselves in a lazy, irrational, stereotypical way of perceiving the world.

I was talking to Dr. Robert Schuller a great man who teaches the world possibility thinking through his famous television show *The Hour or Power* and the awesome books he has written. I asked him what he thought was one of the most important needs humans possess. He told me self-esteem. According to Schuller, for the disappointed, no condition is ever hopeless and helpless!

Bottom line: People with this type of anger require assertiveness training and self-esteem growth.

4

INTERNET & COMPUTER RAGE

No man can think clearly when his fists are clenched.

George Jean Nathan

WHAT'S YOUR ANGER TYPE?

    I'm sure everyone reading this book uses a computer or has had at least one experience using a computer. Moreover, I am sure the majority of readers are connected to the Internet and surf the Web on a regular basis. Did you know the computer you just bought became obsolete within a year or less right after you walked out of the store with it? Well, just knowing that would annoy the heck out of me! You see, the reason why computers become obsolete is technology is changing so fast and the industry is trying to keep up with the advancement rat race. Guess who the rats are chasing after the technological cheese? Well, that would be you and me! We have become part of the process, constantly trying to keep up and stay in sync with change.

    Computer technology is very much like the fast food industry... I want it right here, right now! Most of us do not practice patience. The irony is most industries and homes use computers to do tasks faster and more efficiently. The operative word in the last statement is "faster". The problem becomes how fast is fast enough?

    Recently, I switched over from dial-up Internet to high speed Internet. I was one of those archaic dial-up users who was too lazy to make the switch to high speed. Colleagues and friends kept telling me I'm going to be amazed at the difference between dial-up versus high speed. In fact, I was told "you are going to tell yourself you should have switched much sooner once you see the difference!" Guess what? I made the switch and they were right! The speed was incredibly faster! There was one thing I was left to ponder with high speed. Several high speed users I knew were still complaining that things weren't fast enough. Wow! For me, it was like comparing a ten speed bicycle to a motorcycle. I could see the obvious difference. For them, they had become desensitized to the speed and now needed an even quicker Internet fix!

Internet speed freaks are one thing, but the Internet *"ragers"* are those who displace their dissatisfaction with the speed through forms of aggression and even violence. Here are some of the most common symptoms of Internet rage I have had reported to me while doing research for this type of anger:

- you're waiting for the URL site to change and you're growing impatient
- your screen freezes and you start pounding the mouse or keys
- pop-ups keep appearing on your screen and you

WHAT'S YOUR ANGER TYPE?

start swearing
- your e-mail is overloaded with junk mail and you start cursing
- blind ads are sent to you and you actually reply with nasty e-mails
- you participate in Internet chat to precipitate arguments
- you have to constantly be surfing the Net to get your fix or else you go into withdrawal and get very irritable
- you start stalking others in chat rooms or through their e-mail
- you've actually punched your monitor when things were moving too slow or froze up
- you've actually picked up the monitor and thrown it at the wall or out the window

👍

When doing anger management counseling, I recall one individual was so irate when their screen froze, that they picked up their monitor and threw it out a window of an office building. They forgot they were on one of the higher floors and nearly pegged a pedestrian walking below! Now that's Internet rage with attempted manslaughter!

When I was doing research for this book, lack of Internet speed or the computer not functioning faster were the two most common complaints I heard. In fact, those who became aggressive due to lack of speed only made matters worse when they pounded the mouse or the keyboard as it only froze things up and made them angrier. Some actually punched the "older style monitors" breaking finger nails and fingers!

A colleague of mine who is a university professor, teaching in computer technology, actually teaches her classes a "must hands off skill" the first lecture. She instructs students to guard against Internet rage by having them sit on their hands after clicking the mouse twice. Anymore than twice she asserts is only adding to the computer freezing up and there being further frustration. "Hands under your glutes" is her favorite line! It might be one of the harder things to do, resisting the urge to click the heck out of the mouse. The constant clicking however becomes a precursor to your frustration and anger.

TELEMARKETERS

A similar frustrating technological occurrence which irritates many people are telemarketers, those who phone you at home and try to sell you something. What is it about telemarketers that upsets you? Most say they are just a nuisance. They hate being called at home and disturbed. I can buy that. If you are like myself, your home is your private domain. I operate under the premise that if I want to purchase something, then I can just look it up in the yellow pages or on the Internet.

For some reason it seems telemarketer calls are on the rise. I have been noticing more calls to my house. This occurrence is something I don't get angry about or lose sleep over as that would be foolish. I believe if the callers are a major concern to you and you are in dire straights to protect whatever sanity you have left, then I would suggest trying the following options which I have learned from interviewing people and speaking to law enforcement officials:

- change your phone number to an unlisted number
- put a block on your phone for all unknown numbers

- call the companies or clearing houses directly and ask that your number be taken off their lists
- screen all your calls through call answer
- screen all your calls through call display
- politely tell marketers you are not interested
- speak another language if you can if they are persistent and keep calling you back (remember, I got this from someone who tried it and claimed it worked!)

👍

Getting flustered and upset every time a telemarketer calls can wreck your day. There is no need to get upset over something you can totally control. Why take it out on your family and guests? Furthermore, why beat up the helpless phone? I am sure you would rather spend your money other ways instead of constantly replacing broken phones!

5

ADDICTIVE ANGER

Anger as soon as fed is dead. 'Tis starving makes it fat.

Emily Dickinson

WHAT'S YOUR ANGER TYPE?

As you are reading this, how would you respond to the following statements? I have a hard time living my life in moderation? I get bored quite easily and I always need something or someone to create excitement for me? I am the type of person who loves to take risks. I like to live on the edge! I get very depressed and suffer mood swings unless I am doing something stimulating. I love the intense rush that comes with getting angry! I sometimes get into fights, verbal or physical because it gives me a sense of power and mastery over others. The adrenaline rush I get from my anger is better than any stimulating drug. Getting angry is better than sex!

If you answered yes to any of these statements or scored high in this section of the anger test, then you would be considered to possess Addictive Anger. As this type of anger implies, anger becomes very much like a substance or "addiction" for the individual. Anger becomes a vice because it provides you with one or more of the following feelings:
- gives a sense of instant gratification
- provides relief to negative or depressive moods
- offers some instant reward or reinforcement for the behavior

When I conduct seminars, workshops, support groups and classes on anger management, most individuals snicker or roll their eyes when they are taught about this type of anger. The most common question I am often asked is, "Who in their right mind would want to get high or stoned on anger?" That is a very fair question. I am going to give you three scenarios where you might see this type of anger used or precipitated.

👍

Scenario #1

There are some professional sports like boxing, football and hockey where fighting and aggression are expected and encouraged. Ever heard of the famous hockey expression? Last night I went to a fight and a hockey game broke out? If you watch professional hockey, you are well aware each team carries one or two players referred to as "enforcers", "police officers" or "goons". Their chief role is to protect the higher skilled players on their teams by fighting with the "goons" from the other teams they play. This type of player usually receives a minimal amount of ice time, but when they are called upon, they are out on the ice looking for a fight. They get pumped up on the bench as they await their "seek and destroy" mission! Did you know this player is a catalyst for motivating their own team and fans? The fighting creates a frenzy and gets everyone including the fans pumped up! Everyone's adrenaline starts to rush.

Ask a minority of hockey fans and they will tell you they go to the games to see the fights. I have interviewed hockey fans in the past for other assignments I worked on and something really struck me. Many reported to me they welcomed the fights because they were very cathartic for themselves. You see, catharsis means "release" or stress reducer. For these fans, watching two goons pounding it out on the ice was actually stress relieving for them! In fact, some of these same fans said they sometimes wished they could suit up and get out there and toss a few punches!

What is the cause of anger? Boredom and the need for stimulation.
What are the precipitating factors? The need for a high level of arousal and adrenaline rush.

Scenario #2

If you're a movie buff, you are probably familiar with the movie Raging Bull which starred Robert DeNiro as Jake La Motta. This movie portrayed the boxer both in and out of the ring. DeNiro was fantastic in the movie earning him high acclamations. Actor Joe Pesci plays DeNiro's brother Joey La Motta in the movie. As part of his pre-fight rituals, Pesci is ordered by DeNiro to slap him in the face and get him pumped up. DeNiro thrives on this aggression as a means for getting pumped up for his opponents. And guess what? It works! It literally looks like the trainers of roosters at cock fights or pit bulls at dog fights getting their dogs psyched up using aggression. You see this all the time with football players before and during the game endorsing and facilitating aggression. Their own teammates slap them around and yell at them to get them "more angry". It would appear it seems to work as a motivating factor for some athletes. Anger is used as a motivating factor!

What is the cause of anger? The perceived need for an external motivator.

What are the precipitating factors? Looking outside of yourself to satiate boredom, create excitement and fulfill some kind of longing for satisfaction.

<u>Scenario #3</u>

For this example, I will use the Friday night bruiser who likes going to bars to drink and then get into fights. Typically, this is an individual who lacks self-esteem, has come from an abusive family, has a history of being a bully, and believes the best form of communication involves some form of aggression. Years ago, I was working with individuals mandated into anger management counseling because they were arrested for severe acts of aggression. What I found most disturbing is that these individuals premeditated their Friday night fights. They purposely drank because they knew it would make them more aggressive and want to fight. In fact, I recall one individual telling me he would go to bars on the weekends when he knew they would be busy because he knew someone would bump into him and this would precipitate his anger and lead him into wanting to fight. When I asked him what would possess anyone *to want to get into a fight and possibly hurt someone badly or get hurt his simple response to me was "the rush"!*

What is the cause of anger? Loneliness and boredom.
What are the precipitating factors? The need for attention and recognition.

Addictive anger for some literally becomes their vice. Part of my career involves working in the field of addictions both as a practitioner and as a professor. I find many individuals with addictions have extreme difficulty living their lives in moderation. Their lives are never in proper balance. Over the years I have learned that some people really do possess what are called "addictive" personalities. I believe they are socialized at an early age, by parents or someone close to them to become addictive by nature. They may have witnessed loved ones around them with addictions and they followed in their footsteps.

Have you ever heard the term "dry drunk"? This often times refers to the individual who is in recovery for alcoholism or another substance and begins behaving obsessively or compulsively in some other form. Another more acceptable "vice", perhaps excessive attendance to support groups/counseling or religious fundamentalism becomes the substitute for their drinking or drugging. In essence, they have controlled their substance use, but their addictive personality has not been modified.

Individuals with addictive anger are perhaps in some ways like "dry drunks". They are very addictive in their nature and need something outside of themselves to stimulate their personalities. Much like a compulsive gambler who requires slot machines, card tables, roulette wheels or bingos to provide them with an adrenaline rush, the addictive anger type requires conflict leading to aggression to satiate their thirst for adrenaline. It has been said to me a number of times by individuals possessing this anger type that if they weren't getting into fights all the time, they would be bored as hell! In fact, I have had some individuals actually tell me if they weren't raging all the time, then they would have to find a stimulant such as cocaine, crack or ephedrine to provide them with this "superhuman" adrenaline rush they get.

Some time ago I asked Dr. William Glasser, the creator of Reality Therapy for his view on addiction. He asserted something very profound. He believes addiction separates you from people. You find happiness with people and being around them. On the other hand, pleasure which you find in addiction is usually without people. Is it any wonder your anger pushes people away or you find yourself alone?

People with addictive anger need to find respectable, social activities, events and means to satisfy their boredom.

6

PETRIFIED ANGER

For every minute you remain angry, you give up sixty seconds of peace of mind.

Ralph Waldo Emerson

WHAT'S YOUR ANGER TYPE?

Here is a simple nature lesson to shed some light on petrified anger and how similar it is to wood. So imagine if you will a healthy tree standing growing in the forest. It rests beside the waters edge. The tree is functioning and productive. One day the tree becomes stressed out with a disease which persists for a prolonged period of time. Its ability to function weakens and insects, sensing this, start to feed on the tree until it eventually dies. Over the years the roots of the tree eventually rot out and the tree topples over into the river. The fallen trunk and branches get swept away until it winds up in the bottom of the lake where over the years it becomes petrified. Mother Nature preserves the tree through petrification. All things being equal, this tree will in essence lie fixed in that state at the bottom of the lake for countless years. Aquarium owners who have petrified drift wood in their aquariums can relate to what I am talking about!

You are probably asking yourself at this point, what the heck does petrified driftwood have to do with anger? Simple! Petrified wood undergoes the same kind of process petrified anger follows. Over a period of time, behaviors, attitudes and personalities become solidified and preserved.

Imagine you are the tree. You function healthy and

normal as a child. Everything seems to be good. One day you are forced to deal with unwanted stresses and negativity. Someone does something bad to you or hurts you in such as way it effects your life. You perceive the event as very bad. You believe this situation has caused you prolonged or permanent harm. The experience has left you feeling negative, cynical and hopeless. In fact, you feel sickened by the event or *"diseased"*. You relive the event in your mind over and over. This further facilitates your negative perception of what happened to you. This only makes you angrier. This feeds your irrational thought process, insidiously eating away at you like a disease. Your thought process toward this event and similar ones becomes automatic. Consequently, it becomes solidified or "petrified" like the tree trunk at the bottom of the lake. Over a period of time you have formed a biased perception of what happened and that becomes your truth. Even if your perception of the event was wrong or those involved in causing you hurt tried to make amends, your petrified thought process distorts and shades your perception of the event.

WHAT'S YOUR ANGER TYPE?

Here are three examples of petrified anger at work:

👍

<u>Scenario #1</u>

Your best friend borrows $50 from you. Your friend comes to you and tells you they are a little short of money that week for their bills. You offer to help them by giving them $50. They reluctantly accept the money, but only on the condition they will pay you back in full next month. Being the decent, altruistic person you are you say, "Not a problem, it's only fifty bucks, don't worry about it!" Next month comes and your friend doesn't pay you back. It bothers you they never offered you the money, but you excuse it thinking they are short of money again and they will pay you when they get it. Another couple of weeks pass. A month passes. Now you are really starting to get annoyed. Your friend has not once brought up the subject of the fifty dollars they owe you. You are starting to feel used. Finally, you start to drop hints about the money to your friend. There is no response on their part. Unnerved, you come right out and ask about the money. Your friend responds by telling you they were under the impression you didn't care *about the money or expect to be paid back. This really sends you over the edge. How dare they take you and your money for granted!*

Of course you can't just let bygones be bygones and swallow your pride. You take issue with your friend's complacency. Your friend tries to downplay the situation and even makes light of it which further irritates you. You walk away angry. They may or may not walk away angry as well, but they definitely know where they stand with you. The longer this situation lingers unresolved, the further apart the two of you grow. Even if your friend repaid you the full amount with interest, this would still not be enough to salvage the friendship. The unpaid $50 is no longer the issue as it has become the principle of the matter. You want their most solemn, deepest part of the soul apology which is never going to come.

Instead of forgiving and forgetting, you choose to hold onto the vendetta and wallow in the glory of knowing you were right and your friend was wrong. Basically, you feel it is better to be right and lose a friendship than be the one to cave in and accept your friend's apology. In essence, you grow to enjoy reliving the bitter feelings you have toward your friend over and over.

What is the cause of your anger? Feeling used and taken for granted by your friend.

What are the precipitating factors? Not confronting your friend sooner and being honest with how you feel about them not paying you back. You basically assumed they would pay you back even though you never asked them too. Are you mad at them or more at yourself for not being more assertive in the first place?

<u>Scenario #2</u>

Your family and people of that country were victims of war crimes committed against them decades ago. The wrong doers of the heinous crimes have been brought to justice, some no longer living. You have never resolved the inner conflict and bitterness toward the race of people who committed these crimes.

Now when someone of that specific race tries to get friendly with you, you ignore them. You stereotype all people from that race as part-taking in those war crimes. You feel it is most rewarding, perhaps vengeful to hate all people of that race or wish them ill wills. You basically become what you've accused the perpetrators of the crimes and that race of people of being, racists!

What is the cause of your anger? Continued perceived wrongs done to you at the expense of others.
What are the precipitating factors? Your inability to forgive and let go of past transgressions which cannot be undone.

<u>Scenario #3</u>
As a child your father left you, your siblings and your mother to be self-sufficient. You never heard a word from your father for years. You saw how your mother used to cry herself to sleep nights. You saw how she was late with bill payments. You saw how she tried to contact him many times for some financial assistance and emotional support, but he never returned her calls. He wanted no part of any of you. Now you are a young lady, you find it very difficult trusting men. In fact, a couple of the men you were last involved with facilitated newer trust issues. You pushed them away! You have a tendency to not get close to men because you worry about getting burned. Your mantra is; "it is better to error on the side

of caution than trust another man, especially after what your father did to you and your mother." No man will ever hurt you that way again! According to you, "all men are the same!" Your belief system holds that all men are reasonable facsimiles of the father which deserted you. You have never overcome the hurts and disappointments he caused you. Now you carry with you a hardened, bitterness which you displace on men you meet. You have chosen to hate all men!

What is the cause of your anger? Expecting men to be exactly the way you would like them to be and disappointed when they are not.

What are the precipitating factors for your anger? Not forgiving what your father did to you and your family by abandoning you. Instead, you blame and accuse men you meet for being what your father was. You have made all men into psychological carbon copies of your father!

For most individuals, petrified anger becomes second nature. When you ask them how long they have had this anger toward someone in particular, they can usually tell you in great details the times, dates and particulars of what happened. People with petrified anger literally become obsessed with their feelings of anger and hostility. They derive some sense of satisfaction over reliving what happened because it spurs on feelings of rage. In their minds, they believe that by reliving the event, getting angry and feeling hatred toward the "wrong doer" exacts some sort of revenge. Nothing could be further from the truth. While you are reliving the event and getting yourself worked-up, the target of your hostility has more than likely moved on and could care less what happened in the past. I am sure they felt some discomfort, hurt or anger in the beginning, but they have basically chucked it into the "out of sight, out of mind bin". Wake up folks, these people are the ones who sleep well! While you're losing sleep still trying to flog a dead horse, these people are enjoying deep R.E.M. sleep.

Like resistant anger, people with petrified anger lock everything inside of themselves and start to cause themselves unnecessary suffering. If you keep reliving the same event over again, you basically become like an individual who suffers from posttraumatic stress disorder (PTSD). This disorder carries with it some very unpleasant feelings and physical disorders:

- bitterness
- flashbacks
- depression
- anxiety
- fear
- nausea/vomiting
- insomnia
- constant worrying
- irritability
- increased alcohol/drug consumption
- bodily aches and pains
- increased blood pressure
- increased heart rate

    In essence, petrified anger is like a mocked form of PTSD. The individual really truly believes they were victimized, abused or exploited. For some, their distorted reality leads them to believe they were like a "casualty of war", much like an individual who suffers PTSD from serving in the Vietnam or the Persian Gulf war.

    What many individuals don't understand is that by reliving their experiences repetitiously, the mind tricks the body into believing the experience is real. The body reacts accordingly and prepares itself for fight mode. Over a period of time, you actually tax your body by putting it into what Walter Cannon called the "Fight or Flight Syndrome", where you keep creating adrenaline rushes which tax the central nervous system. Given time, the body could actually suffer from what Hans Selye found in his General Adaptation Syndrome model. In a very condensed form, this model asserts that the more we are in this "high state of alert" posturing, the more we drain ourselves and weaken our immune systems possibly causing serious or permanent damage. Perhaps the best way to summarize how this model fits in with petrified anger is as follows:

<u>Event</u> > *Anger* > *Bitterness* > *Relive Experience* > *Elevated Blood Pressure* > *Adrenaline Rush* > *Repeat Cycle Too Many Times* > *Weakened Immune System* > *Exhaustion (mental or physical illness)*

Is it really worth feeling this bitterness toward someone? Does it bring you that much satisfaction in that it could literally age you faster and make you sick? Are you a fan of such shows like The Sopranos or movies like The Godfather or Good Fellas, that vendettas are the only way to settle old scores? Always

WHAT'S YOUR ANGER TYPE?

remember, forgiveness goes along way for everyone involved, mostly you!

7

COMPRESSIVE ANGER

People who fly into a rage always make a bad landing.

Will Rogers

WHAT'S YOUR ANGER TYPE?

If you possess this type of anger, you are a walking time bomb! Three things to know right from the get go: 1) You possess a short fuse, (2) You have a sensitive trigger, and (3) others close to you probably know which buttons to push to get you going.

Earlier in the book I discussed that anger is a normal, healthy emotion that everyone experiences. I also eluded to the point that individuals who "act crazy" when they are angry literally give anger it's negative, maniacal connotation. This is compressive anger! I've had clients, colleagues and friends claiming they go from zero to sixty in 0.001 seconds when they snap! In fact, when I ask them what they are thinking about to get themselves in this dither, they claim they didn't have time to think. They just explode! Of course, this is not true. You have to think about something first before you can create that feeling for yourself. I will however assert there are certain individuals out there who are puppeteers who know exactly what buttons to go after to stimulate you to explode faster if you possess this type of anger.

The following are three scenarios which depict compressive anger. All possess the same element, becoming irrational without first rationalizing.

Scenario #1

You are rushing for work. You are always waiting until the last minute to get things done. What you could have prepared the night before, you put off until the morning. Unforeseen obstacles arise as they usually do and your kids are not co-operating with you. You ask yourself, "why me?" This further fuels your fire as you start to believe everyone is against you. There are some mysterious forces at work purposely trying to make you miserable. You thrive off of this irrational belief process and this precipitates greater frustration. Finally, the kids are off to school and you are on your way to work. If traffic is co-operative, then you will make it to work with 30 seconds to a minute to spare. It looks good. You're going to do it! That was until the train came, the long one I might add. Guess what? For sure you're going to be late for work! You sit and stew in the car, pounding the steering wheel and cursing at the top of your lungs at the engineer.

WHAT'S YOUR ANGER TYPE?

Anger Cause: Frustration

Precipitating Factors: Bad planning, procrastination

Scenario #2

You come home from work. Your teenage son has 4 pairs of shoes strewn about the entrance in your hallway. He is sitting in the living room with his feet propped up on the coffee table. This in itself is enough to ignite your ire. However, there are bigger fish to fry. The night before as well as before going to work in the morning, you asked him to cut the lawn. In fact, it was more of an order you barked out seeing as he didn't cut the lawn the three previous days when asked. You confront him and ask him why the lawn isn't cut, as if you really need an answer. From the time you pulled into the driveway until you saw him seated on the sofa, you couldn't wait to confront him. You didn't have such a great day at work today. It was a matter of time before your fuse was fully lit. Before he even has a chance to give you a reason, you tear into him fiercely. Your blood pressure has risen to its boiling point and the foulest of words start spewing from your mouth. You feel your head getting lighter and hot. Your temple starts beating at a feverish rate. You've gone from zero to sixty in microseconds. This sets the tempo for the rest of your evening as you start yelling at other members of your family. At night's end, you go to bed with a migraine headache and no one wants to talk to you. And one more thing... The lawn never did get cut!

What is the cause of anger: Stress, frustration and disappointment.
Precipitating Factors: Lack of discipline and lack of corrective consequences.

Scenario #3

Heather arrives home from work late. Her husband Anthony inquires as to why she is late. She informs him she stopped for coffee with some of her girlfriends after work to plan for an upcoming baby shower. Anthony is irate she would do that and not come home and have dinner ready for the kids. Anthony starts yelling at her demanding her place is in the home to support her family. Anthony accuses her of not caring for the kids or him. He asserts she does this on purpose to defy *him. In the past he has had a history of abusing Heather both verbally and physically. Recently, he reluctantly agreed to her working again after she threatened to leave him. Anthony believes she is "taking advantage" of her freedom. Before they discuss the situation any further, Anthony is already grabbing her arm!*

What is the cause of anger? Anthony's irrational beliefs. What are the precipitating factors? Lack of communication, unrealistic expectations, irrational and rigid thinking.

Compressive anger is perhaps one of the most serious anger types as it has the propensity to cause immediate harm. The hallmark of compressive anger is individuals lose their abilities to rationalize and control the situation. In fact, this type of anger usually causes the individual to lose control of themselves as well as the situation they are in. The key ingredients in this anger are violence and aggression, two emotions which eventually lead to irreparable damage.

Over the years I have worked with many clients and couples who possessed this type of anger. This type of anger was very common in domestic violence and battered spouse syndrome. I believe all forms of violence are wrong and should not be tolerated. No one should stay in abusive relationships as they are not only harmful to the victim, but to the children who witness this abuse as well. Typically, domestic abusers possess compressive anger and their spouse usually becomes the target of their projected low self-esteem and inadequacies. More often than not, abusers come from abusive dysfunctional families themselves. They were either a victim of abuse or watched one parent abuse the other. They irrationally learned aggression solves problems which is wrong!

    In my book *Why Women Want What They Can't Have*, I discuss why people stay in abusive relationships and the dynamics involved. The book focuses on Object Relations Cycle and the whole gambit of abuse. To quickly summarize the abuse, in many cases men tend to be the physical abusers and women use emotional abuse, or push their mate's buttons to antagonize the abuse. This may sound absolutely ludicrous, and I am in no way saying abused women seek abuse or ask for it, but many become patterned participators in the cycle of abuse. They realize their mates are bigger and stronger. The only damage some can do is emotionally aggravate/abuse to retaliate. In most domestic abuse situations, the cycle literally plays like a broken record which follows the same repetitious script. She knows he has a short fuse and intentionally or unintentionally provokes him to eruption. Once he becomes abusive, she mocks him and points out, "see, you never changed, you still pick on women", or "wow, it takes a lot of courage to beat on a helpless woman." This is further likely to frustrate his already weakened ego state and perpetuate further violence.

I spoke with Dr. Susan Weitzman, author of the great book *Not To People Like Us!* You might have seen Weitzman discussing her book on Oprah. Her book focuses on domestic abuse seen in upper class families. She told me something which reaffirmed my own findings. Men can become habituated to abusing their wives, while their wives can become habituated to certain lifestyles and use excuses to justify the abuse.

People with compressive anger need to take anger management counseling, workshops, or support groups in order to identify their triggers and nip "trigger manipulation" in the bud. Most people with compressive anger most likely identify certain people in their lives or situations as their triggers. Unfortunately, most will blame the situation or the person rather than identifying their own interpretation and irrational belief system as the core problem. Once you can identify what your triggers are, then you can interpret your irrational thinking patterns. The key is to learn to respond differently to the people or situations which you believe provoke you.

If you recall, most people with compressive anger problems will assert their anger happens too fast, from zero to sixty in microseconds! They contend they don't have time to think, they just explode! Quite the opposite is true. You do have time to think as it is your perception of the situation first, then your irrational thinking process (albeit fast) which leads you to feeling anger. I do believe some individuals learn this anger like a skill or talent through repetition and are capable of putting minimal mental effort to get them to that level of anger. Stereotypes are short-cuts to perceptions. Moreover, they are lazy perceptions. Rather than look at each situation and individual differently each time, you start to stereotype similar situations you're in or individuals you see often. You expect them to be the same and behave the same, thus stimulating your preconceived notions for how you will respond.

In abusive relationships, both parties play the anger and abuse out as if they were reciting the same script over and over again. In fact, many of my former clients would say it started the same way, the plot was the same and the outcome was predictable. People can master their compressive anger much like a musician mastering the piano, a golfer perfecting their swing or smoker lighting a cigarette! It becomes second nature to them with minimal discriminating thought invested.

8

JEALOUSY

♋

Anger and jealousy can no more bear to lose sight of their objects than love.

George Eliot

Besides being one of the seven deadly sins listed in the Bible, jealousy is also a type of anger some people possess. Jealousy when left unchecked and allowed to progress, could escalate into other anger types such as petrified and compressive. Individuals with jealousy anger develop it through repetitious experiences of rejection, betrayal and loss. Many of their experiences occurred very early on in life when they experienced some kind of abandonment/rejection from a parent, or they experienced personal loss, perhaps the death of a loved one. Some individuals may have been raised in a lower class environment where nice clothing, shoes, toys and opportunities were hard to come by and other children who were more fortunate, made fun of them and belittled them. This could have led to rejection by their peers, or made them feel unwanted and worthless.

The hallmark of jealousy anger is perceived ownership and possession. The individual with jealousy has learned to try to possess whatever comes into their life. Many individuals who have jealousy issues usually live their lives in fear of rejection or loss. The pain of losing someone or being rejected early on in life created deep wounds which never healed. Individuals are also likely to have never forgiven those who have wronged them in the past and this has only caused the wound of jealousy to fester deeper.

These are some of the negative attributes associated with jealousy:

- Angered by people more successful than you.
- Believes the world owes you something.
- Believes there is some higher power in control who manipulates people like puppets on a string.
- Believes loyalty exists to one person only.
- Always believes in reciprocity when you do something for another person.
- Needs to be the focal point of attention from partners and best friends.
- Keeps a running score card of favors done for others.
- Possesses irrational beliefs where you believe people are conspiring to hurt you or use you.
- Fears getting close to others due to fear or rejection.
- Possessiveness of loved ones or things you own.
- Fears commitment.
- Checking and stalking behaviors of those you are currently involved with or former relationships.
- Uses abusive and controlling behaviors.

WHAT'S YOUR ANGER TYPE?

There is a psychological term listed in the DSM-IV, the medical bible called obsessive compulsive disorder. People with the disorder obsess over thoughts which create stress and frustration. They may also engage in obsessing behaviors such as checking, washing, etc., to alleviate their tensions. This by no means is a form of jealousy anger. In fact, I have counseled clients possessing Obsessive Compulsive Personality Disorder which is found in the DSM-IV under personality disorders. The hallmark of this personality disorder diagnoses the individual with traits which include; perfectionism, controlling behaviors, possession and irrational jealousy. In most cases, individuals with this personality disorder did in fact experience rejection and loss early on in life, along with other factors which led to their developing this disorder. Moreover, people with this disorder usually do possess jealousy anger!

Here are some examples which illustrate jealousy anger:

<u>Scenario #1</u>

Ten year old Allan gets reprimanded by his fifth grade school teacher for punching a classmate who took the atlas from Allan's desk. The atlas belongs to the classroom and Allan had used the book to find some destinations for a class project he was working on. He was finished with the book, but left it on his desk. The student asked Allan if he could use the atlas and Allan said no. Observing Allan away from the desk, working on something else, the student thought he would take the book and quickly look up something and return the book to the desk before Allan noticed. When sent to the principle's office, it was acknowledged in Allan's file he had a history of stealing small articles from other students as well as hoarding.

What is the cause of Allan's anger? Jealousy
What are the precipitating factors? Feeling inadequate, low self-esteem, feeling the need for power.

WHAT'S YOUR ANGER TYPE?

Scenario #2

After repeated marital counseling attempts and interventions, Lucy has finally decided to leave her husband Tim. The biggest complaint Lucy has had about Tim throughout their four years together is he never shares his feelings with her and there is little, if any communication in their marriage. Lucy has voiced her need for emotional intimacy repeatedly, but Tim has told her that is "not him" and he is not into that "pop psychology crap". Frustrated, Lucy has consciously made the decision to move on with her life. Acknowledging the severity of the situation this time, Tim has initiated going for marital counseling. Lucy has told him it is too late for that! Tim tells her he will do whatever counseling it takes to save their marriage and also promises to change. Lucy points out that has been his common element of manipulation throughout their four years, that whenever she threatens to leave, he promises to change. Unfortunately, the "changes" last long enough to appease her and for him to become complacent again in the relationship. After repeated attempts to salvage the marriage, Tim realizes she is gone for good his time. A year has past and Tim is still stalking her! Lucy started dating someone only to have him dump her because he was afraid of the threats Tim was making. Tim keeps telling her he has changed and to "please give me one last chance"!

What is the cause of Tim's anger? Rejection, feeling abandoned, feeling betrayed.
What are the precipitating factors? Perhaps rejection in childhood from parents, loved ones or repeated failed relationships with women he has been intimate with in the past.

<u>Scenario #3</u>

    Marty works at a blue collar job and pulls in an average income. He is married with two children. They live next door to the Johnson's. Mr. Johnson is professionally employed and "only buys" the best for his family. The Johnson kids are always bragging to Marty's kids about what their parents bought them. Marty's own wife and children have sarcastically rubbed it in his face that they wished they had more, or were rich. Deep down, this really bothers Marty. He wishes he could offer them more, but the opportunity to earn a higher income is just not in the cards. Most of his income goes toward their mortgage and bills and also toward, "keeping up with the Johnsons". Marty's wife has not worked in four years since their daughter was born. She believes the man should be the bread winner in the family and refuses to go back to work. She really believes it is up to Marty to give her and the kids a life comparable to the Johnson family. On several occasions, Marty has suggested they move into a more modest house which would allow them to get out of debt faster. His wife does not agree. Mr. Johnson just purchased a top of the line car and Marty came home to see his wife and son enamored with the car. At the dinner table that night, his wife starts asking when they will buy a new car. Frustrated and fed up, Marty leaves the table and takes off for a few hours. He has a couple of drinks at a local bar close to home. Arriving home close to midnight, he ogles the new car in the Johnson driveway. He notices all the lights are off in their house. They must be sleeping. Just before going into his house, he picks up a rock from his flower bed and throws it as hard as he can at the car. He hits it dead on and the alarm sounds. He disappears into the house as the lights in the Johnson house come on.

What is the cause of Marty's anger? Envy and jealousy.

What are the precipitating factors? Financial stress, emotional stress and frustration.

Individuals with this anger type feel inadequate about themselves much of the time. They are most likely comparing themselves to others they wish they were like, or wishing for what others have. Interestingly, they would deny ever wanting to be like anyone else. In fact, they put down those they most want to be like. They criticize other peoples' success, acquired possessions, usually demeaning anything positive or beautiful about them. Some people with jealousy anger are likely to use putdowns in front of people to try and make themselves look better.

Perhaps the worst place to see jealousy anger rearing its ugly head is after the breakup of a relationship. When the individual with jealousy gets rejected and feels spurned, they will go to great lengths to try and salvage the relationship. It is during this time the individual will try to bargain, compromise and promise to change in order to be given one more chance. When the final dissolution of the marriage becomes obvious to the "rejected", they are unwilling to accept the outcome. They believe if they "could just get their ex-mate to listen and give them another chance", things would work out. They begin pressuring their ex-mate for "another chance" further pushing them away. As their mate pulls further away, they start to pursue them, believing persistence produces romance. What they believe to be romantic often times becomes stalking behaviors, harassment and aggression. This only alienates their estranged spouse more, causing fear and resentment. When you examine domestic cases where "peace bonds" or restraining orders have been issued, the perpetrator usually possesses jealousy anger.

Individuals with jealousy anger really do need counseling, support groups or courses which will enhance self-esteem building. Moreover, those with unresolved issues stemming from childhood probably require more intense therapy to reprogram their irrational thinking tendencies.

9

ROAD RAGE

In times of great stress or adversity, it's always best to keep busy, to plow your anger and your energy into something positive.

Lee Iacocca

WHAT'S YOUR ANGER TYPE?

Over the last decade so much has been made about road rage. I have been asked by members of police forces I have worked with as to why I think the number of road rage incidents has increased and continues to increase? I believe there are a number of reasons we are seeing the number of enraged drivers losing it on road ways:

- increases in the number of drivers
- city populations are growing
- people are becoming lazy drivers in that they take for granted the rules of the road and don't signal
- lack of courtesy to other drivers
- we live in an instant gratification society where we are always rushing
- bad time management leading to lateness/rushing
- influx of immigrants who abide according to their own cultural driving norms
- multi-tasking while driving: talking on the phone, smoking, eating/drinking, watching television, reading the paper, putting on make-up, shaving, arguing with children

- a greater number of larger/taller vehicles which you can't see around: SUV's, pick-up trucks and vans
- lack of law enforcement for traffic violators
- too many places to get too in a short period of time
- simply put, just bad drivers

👍

The most common complaint I usually hear is that the reason road rage occurs is due to the age of the driver. Notice I didn't list this above? I don't believe the age of the driver has anything to do with road rage. I often hear young drivers complaining about seniors driving too slow or erratically. On the other hand, I hear elder drivers complain that younger drivers drive too fast or too recklessly! I also hear women complain about men driving without any courtesy or sensitivity. Conversely, I hear men complain female-drivers multi-task which causes erratic driving. I have also heard that it's only members of a certain culture or country which are the worst drivers which I also don't buy! There are a number of reasons which lead to poor driving and eventually to road rage.

After speaking with individuals in law enforcement, particularly highway and traffic divisions, I've compiled a list of traffic infractions which can lead to road rage or are episodes of road rage. When you drive, if you are guilty of committing any of these offenses, you might be considered a *"road rager"*!

Do you:

1) Follow too closely vehicles in front of you?
2) Fail to signal when changing lanes?
3) Drive too fast, way above the speed limit?
4) Flash your high beams at other drivers who go too slow in front of you?
5) Cut people off intentionally?
6) Purposely go too slow or keep braking to annoy drivers behind you?
7) Purposely speed up to prevent other drivers from passing you?
8) Run amber and red lights?
9) Ignore the flashing lights/stop signs of school buses?
10) Fail to pull over when an EMS vehicle has its lights flashing?

11) Drive too slow in the fast lane/passing lane on the highway?

12) Make obscene gestures or yell at other drivers?

13) Throw your trash/litter out the window?

14) Multi-task instead of paying attention to the road when driving?

15) Drive an unsafe vehicle, or vehicle which pollutes the air?

16) Drive without a seat belt?

17) Drive recklessly on purpose to impress passengers?

18) Engage in races with other drivers while putting others at risk?

19) Drive while intoxicated or too tried?

20) Follow drivers who have wronged you to try and even the score, or confront them by arguing or fighting?

21) Throw objects or spit at other vehicles?

22) Chase after someone while calling the police to report them?

23) Threaten other drivers with a weapon?

24) Follow the other driver home or to a parking lot and cause damage to their vehicle while they are way from it?

25) Purchase a larger vehicle with the sole purpose of intimidating other drivers?

If you answered yes to several of these questions, then you might consider yourself a *"road rager"!*

Some individuals I interviewed report becoming a whole different personality when they get behind the wheel of their car. In fact, some have told me they feel more powerful and indestructible. They crank up the volume on the radio and they feel ready to conquer the Indy 500! Also, I have had some drivers tell me they feel a certain anonymity or disassociation from themselves when they climb into their vehicles. This is very true for those who have tinted or blackened windows where you can't see into their vehicles.

Some drivers reported "feeling trapped" as their prime catalysts. They can't tolerate being caught in traffic jams which creates discomfort. Many times when people are already late for appointments, bumper to bumper traffic only adds to their frustration and may spill out into them aggressing. Drivers operating smaller cars often complain about larger vehicles and trucks when they are stuck in traffic. Many say the most annoying aspect of their experience is their inability to see around the large vehicle in front of them. Furthermore, others complain being unable to see around a large vehicle engaged in stop and go traffic becomes tedious due to the sudden stops. This experience sends individuals into irate states, some actually challenging transport trucks in their little sedans!

Here are a couple of examples of road rage in action. Perhaps you can relate to one or all of them?

👍

<u>Scenario #1</u>

You are driving in the fast lane of the highway on route to your cottage. The weekend finally arrives and you make tracks. The trip starts out good until you hit the main arteries of the highway where traffic gets congested. This will easily delay your arrival time by at least an hour. This frustrates you as it is usually a four hour trip. Your kids in the back seat start complaining that they are "bored". The refrain of "Are we there yet?" starts up. This starts to get under your skin, *especially listening to your wife repetitively sighing and telling them to shut up. Finally, there is a bit of a break in the traffic. You put the foot to the metal and try to make up for lost time. It looks like clear sailing in front of you. You worry this might not last long, that there might be further congestion down the road so you go even faster. Your wife warns you about your speed and you tell her to mind her own business. Fifteen minutes later, a highway ranger tags you for speeding. You were caught doing way above the maximum speed. You become infuriated that you got caught! You are even more upset with the highway ranger for not being more sympathetic to your being stuck in traffic for nearly an hour. You flunk the attitude test with the cop and he charges you to the maximum!*

What is the cause of the anger? Road rage caused by stress and frustration.
What were the precipitating factors? Feeling righteously justified to speed because the world owed you for the traffic jam which inconvenienced your vacation.

Scenario #2

It's holiday season and you wait until the last minute to do your gift buying. Definitely, not in the holiday spirit, you force yourself to go to the shopping mall. Pick a number! Just trying to find a parking place is impossible. Finally, you see a car pulling out and you race to the spot. You arrive at exactly the same moment as another driver. You both position your cars toward the spot so neither one of you can get in. You start honking at one another and begin making obscene gestures. Cars are starting to line up as they try to pass. These drivers are now getting upset. You won't budge, neither will the other driver. Finally, mall security comes and asks both of you to get out of your cars. You both reluctantly agree. Security asks one of you to step down and find another spot. Neither of you will agree to this. There is no way you will give up "your" coveted spot! After ten more minutes of this absurd behavior, a police officer arrives at the scene. You are both informed neither one of you will get the spot. This makes you totally irate and you start complaining to the police officer. You start yelling at the other driver and making threats. Before you know it, you are being charged with uttering threats, disturbing the peace and *obstructing justice! All in the name of a parking spot.*

What is the cause of the anger? *Believing that another driver showed no respect for you.*
What were the precipitating factor? *Feeling cheated/robbed of the spot, frustrated from the traffic in the parking lot and believing others didn't respect your value as a human being.*

<u>Scenario #3</u>

You are driving on the highway and it seems everyone is doing at least ten miles an hour over the speed limit. The highway is three lanes wide and you keep pace with the flow. You are on your way to work which normally takes a half hour but you think you can shave ten minutes off your arrival time. A sports car flies past you as do two others. You decide to keep pace with them and begin following behind. Easily, they are twenty miles an hour over the speed limit. There are at least five cars now in front of you as you trail behind. Suddenly, out of nowhere you see sirens flashing behind you. You pull into the right hand lane expecting the cop to drive past you and ticket one of the sports cars. As you move into the right lane, so *does the cop. It is you who gets ticketed! You angrily start yelling at the cop for pulling you over. You plead, "How come those cars going a lot faster weren't caught first?" The cop says nothing other than you were going well over the speed limit and breaking the law and you are the one getting the ticket. After all is said and done, you get back into your car and onto the highway, purposely driving the speed limit in the fast lane and forcing traffic to pass you.*

What is the cause of the anger? Believing you were wrongly ticketed and mistreated.
What are the precipitating factors? Irrationally believing that if other people break the law then it must be okay and that you are no longer accountable. Minimizing the wrong doing you were doing and maximizing the same wrong others were doing.

With all the technological advances and safety features in motor vehicles, traffic fatalities are not diminishing. In fact, it seems that the rates for violating laws is increasing. One of the greatest concerns I have observed, as have many traffic enforcement officials is the growing number of people running not just amber lights, but red lights! I have interviewed people I know who run amber lights and asked them why? Their responses are startling! Some asserted they had been hit from behind in the past because they were in fact slowing down to stop for an amber light. The driver behind had expected them to run the amber light so they didn't even try to slow down. The next thing they knew, the driver behind them was glued to their bumper! Some people have consciously or unconsciously set their minds to this apprehension and hold no qualms about running the light. A colleague and friend of mine who is a cop made an interesting observation. When pulling over drivers who had run amber lights and red lights, he got these responses. Red light violators said, "I'm sorry, I know I did wrong by running that light! Please go easy on me." Conversely, amber light violators most often reported the following, "It was only yellow and thought I could beat it before it turned red!" Yellow means stop too at traffic lights!

    I predict in the near future, there will be more defensive driving classes, driving skills classes and stiffer penalties for road rage offenders. If fatalities continue to increase and insurance premiums go up, society will have no choice other than re-educate people to improve their driving skills.

10

CONFLICTUAL ANGER

Anger is never without an argument, but seldom with a good one.

George Saville

WHAT'S YOUR ANGER TYPE?

Would you consider yourself to be an over-analytical person? Are you always beating things to death until you get the answer you want? Most times are you still not satisfied with the answer? Has anyone ever referred to you as a fault finder? Are you able to find the black cloud in the rainbow? Do you make mountains out of mole hills? Do you enjoy getting into arguments and disagreements with others because this gives you a sense of power and control? If you answered yes to one or more of these statements then you might be an individual who possesses conflictual anger!

The trademark of this type of anger is feeling a sense of inferiority. Psychoanalyst Alfred Adler referred to individuals who have low self-esteem, lack communication skills and possess poor social skills as being those most likely to possess this complex. Generally, people feeling like outcasts from society are likely to feel inferior. This complex was created early in life when they were rejected by their parents, families, were part of dysfunctional families, or felt rejected by society. They felt they did not fit in and started to develop feelings of alienation and even isolation. Many people who go through this process become extremely passive and may even become depressed. Some develop a sense of learned helplessness and this facilitates the onset of depression and hopelessness.

Some individuals possessing inferiority complexes grow frustrated and discontent with their current situations. Rather than remain in a helpless and hopeless mindset, they learn to overcome these passive feelings by replacing them with more aggressive feelings. These aggressive feelings create an altogether new complex known as the superiority complex. Individuals learn how to overcome their sense of helplessness and rejection by developing a more aggressive thinking style. They become fed-up with the fact they were rejected early on in life. They despise further rejection! Instead of feeling victimized, they learn to be the *"rejectors"*. If they could reject others first, before they get rejected, then they would no longer feel helpless and worthless. Some learned to "even up the score" by being a bully. They would abuse or reject others first before it could be done to them. Of course, many of these individuals actually misperceived others' intentions. Others could have been intending the best, but because of repeated rejection, the one rejected starts perceiving all situations as being the same!

The key element in this type of anger is a sense of feeling powerful through the creation of arguments, conflicts and disagreements. The individual possesses some degree of a superiority complex because of their previous/present feelings of inferiority and they engage others in arguments as a means of flexing their superiority. I have had colleagues in the world of law enforcement assert that some individuals wish to become cops because it would give them a sense of power and authority they have never felt. They would be able to use their badge as an extension of their manhood. One police officer I know has referred to this as "little, big man syndrome". I have even heard stories from others who, wear shirts one size too small to make them appear larger, or wear shirts one or two sizes bigger so the label on the shirt makes them appear larger than they are! Obviously, this is taking the complex one step too far!

Here are some examples which demonstrate how individuals display conflictual anger. Perhaps you can see some of these traits within yourself.

👍

Scenario #1

You are a member of the school board and regularly

expected to attend staff meetings. After the last meeting, the principle of the school called you into his office to discuss some concerns. The main issue was some fellow teachers accused you of having hidden agendas and purposely creating arguments and disagreements, even over the smallest of issues. For years, you have felt that no one really listens to you. And when you do make your point known, no one takes you seriously. You find others, especially at these staff meetings who make stupid suggestions which are always getting validated by other teachers. Lately, since challenging their suggestions and as one teacher put it, "being the stick in the mud", it seems your colleagues now find you to be argumentative. In closing your meeting with the principle, he points out that from his own observations, you are probably alienating your colleagues and they are probably going to pull further way from you.

What is the cause of the anger? Feeling inferior to your peers. What are the precipitating factors? Believing your peers think they are better than you and also holding the perception if the former statement is true, then this must make you worthless. All is based on irrational thinking!

WHAT'S YOUR ANGER TYPE?

Scenario #2

You write editorials to your local newspaper on a weekly basis. Everyone in your community knows who you are from reading your editorials. Unfortunately, you are getting known as a "fault finder" with everything. It seems all of your editorials come across as attacks on members in political offices and government expenditures. Over the last year, you have applied for several jobs and no one is calling you in for interviews. In fact, some of the positions you applied for were being advertised by the same government officials you had lambasted in the newspapers. You call the places you have applied too to see how they can shed insights as to how you might qualify for a job, but they are not returning your phone calls. This makes you more irate and you criticize the city even further in your new editorials.

What is the cause of the anger? Being rejected. This inflames your elevated sense of self-worth.
What are the precipitating factors? Frustration over being rejected which was created by your own doing.

Scenario #3

Before going to work, you and your wife had an argument over the smallest of things. In fact, your wife tells you she can't even remember how the argument even started. You remember though! Before leaving the house, you still take another jab at getting in the last word. Neither of you have spoken throughout the entire day. As you arrive home, you see her car parked in the driveway. You are fumed over the fact that she never called you at work to say hi. You begin telling yourself she believes you were wrong and that she was in the right, thus winning the argument. This starts to really get you mad. How dare she not have the decency to at least call you at work! You grow more infuriated! You are already planning for the argument you will start once you get in the house. You drive around the block a couple of times planning your argument and rebuttal.

What is the cause of the anger? Your sense of self-righteousness, and fear of being wrong.
What were the precipitating factors? Perhaps repeated failures in the past, feeling worthless and believing if you make a mistake it would mean not only failing in that situation, but also

failing as a person.

Conflictual anger has its roots in failures experienced early on in life which were either magnified by parents, teachers or caregivers. You internalized the failure as being representative of yourself as a person. You may have learned from parental disputes that solutions did arise from fighting, albeit they were dysfunctional most times. You were taught to believe that being abrasive or argumentative produces results. Ever heard the expression, "the squeaky wheel always gets oiled"? For this type of anger, I am not just referring to the squeaky wheel, rather the entire rusting axel!

Let me ask you a question. Is it better to be wrong and still have friends and people like you, or are you of the mindset that it is better to be right and win arguments with the risk of alienating people? Most people with conflictual anger fall into the second part of the question. They trick themselves into believing they would actually admit their mistakes when they are wrong. What feeds their anger is their inability to accept and believe they could be wrong! To accept being wrong would mean they are bad people who make stupid decisions. If this is the case, then this must make them stupid people! Doesn't this line of logic sound ridiculous? It is! This however has become the thinking process for the individual with conflictual anger.

They need to stop being too critical of themselves and perceiving others as always judging their performances. If an actor was to play a role in a movie which absolutely stunk, would this make them a bad actor? Definitely not! It was only a single event. In reality, this shouldn't make or break the person. Furthermore, say the actor's performances in all of the movies they appeared in stunk, does this make them a bad person overall? Definitely not! You have to separate the person from their performance. There is no such thing as a bad person. There are people who do bad things. Individuals with this anger type need to distinguish between these two states and remove the "perfectionist" pressures they are placing on themselves and others. Remember, discussions can be just discussions. They do not always have to become arguments!

11

HABITUAL ANGER

☹

Resentment is like taking poison and waiting for the other person to die.

Malachy McCourt

Has anyone close to you ever told you that you seem angry most of the time? Perhaps all of the time? Do you feel angry most of the day almost every day? Do you tend to watch a lot of movies which have as their central theme vengeance, aggression and violence? Does this act as a catharsis for you, helping you relieve your own feelings of aggression? Do you tend to have recurrent dreams or similar dreams which have as their message, anger and violence? Do you seem to wake up angry each day and go to bed each night feeling angry? Well, these are some of the most common attributes for possessing habitual anger!

As its name implies, habitual anger is a habit. For this person, anger becomes a habit. It is no different from the person who makes happiness, joy and peace their chosen feelings. This type of anger usually started early in life. It persisted into teenage years because of repetition. It eventually stuck because the candidate possessing this anger never challenged themselves to acknowledge it or change it. Habitual anger may have become a conditioned response to witnessing parents and caregivers who were angry most of the time. You might have grown up in a very depressed environment where dysfunction was the norm. Having experienced this type of negativity and pessimism, it could have led you to repeated frustrations. Ultimately, this culminated in you becoming an angry person. Habitual anger is very easy to see in others when you are on the outside looking in. If you are on the inside looking out, when others point your anger out to you, it only infuriates you. Like pouring gasoline on a fire, your habitual anger consumes you that much more!

Here are some examples where habitual anger is most often seen. If you possess habitual anger, do you see yourself in any of these situations?

👍

<u>Scenario #1</u>

You got to bed late last night. You were tired, but couldn't sleep. It could have been drinking the two cups of coffee close to bed time. You tossed and turned most of the night. Finally, just when you fell asleep, you were rudely awakened by your blaring clock radio. And to make matters worst, the song which woke you is one you absolutely despise! It's time to get up and get ready for work. You rush to put out

WHAT'S YOUR ANGER TYPE?

your garbage which you should have put out the night before. As you dump the garbage off at the street, your smiling friendly neighbor wishes you a good morning. Seeing your neighbor all bright and cheery annoys you more. What gives them the right to be so happy this morning? You get in the car and drive to work. Everyone is either driving too slow or too fast. You believe some are purposely trying to make you late for work. Every radio station is playing the same "garbage" music, or the damn disk jockeys are all talking blather which totally annoys you! You smile at another co-worker as you pull into the parking lot but they fail to return a smile. This infuriates you. You hold the door open for some people on the way in and there is not so much as a "thank you". You tell yourself people are annoying. You hate them!

What is the cause of your anger? Believing life owes you more and that you are entitled to things being easier.
What are the precipitating factors? Stress and frustration caused by negative perceptions and expectancies of other people.

Scenario #2

You get the newspaper first thing in the morning and read the headlines. Every headline appears to be screaming doom and gloom. You read about what the government is doing and what it isn't doing. This infuriates you. You decide to save some time getting ready for work so you turn on the television to get more informed about what is going on in the world. It seems three out of every four news captions are either discussing wars, acts of terrorism or problems with the economy. It seems the world is full of nothing but chaos and disarray. You start to think to yourself about the dead-end job you are going to out of necessity to pay your bills. You ask yourself, "What's the use the government just taxes me to death anyway?" It seems to you everything in life is a waste of time! No matter how hard you try to get ahead you get screwed! The news reaffirms your negative beliefs about people and the world. Your day is wrecked before you've even left the house to start making things happen.

What is the cause of your anger? Seeking out negative affirmations which feed your negative expectations of people and the world.

What are the precipitating factors? Maintaining negative stereotypes and being attracted to negativity which feeds and influences them. Your negative outlook is like a magnet which attracts or seeks out like-minded themes.

<u>Scenario #3</u>

You hate the way people drive. It makes you angry that bad things are always happening to innocent people. You hate paying taxes. You believe the government are crooks. Waiting in lines at grocery stores or gas pumps annoys you. It annoys you when delivery people don't deliver things on time. Your neighbor's garbage blew on your lawn, you could kill him! Your satellite receiver went down, man you're miffed! The damn weather! It rains or snows all the time. People stare at you in restaurants when you are eating. How dare they? And if that isn't enough, your food is always over-cooked or cold. You go to have a bath and there's not enough hot water. Damn the kids outside having fun and screaming! They are so annoying. Your flight has been delayed due to inclement weather. Damn *pilot! No one co-operates with you. It seems everyone is against you.*

What is the cause of your anger? Being a fault finder and expecting everything to be the way you like it.
What are the precipitating factors? Setting yourself up or others to fail or fall short of the mark. You personalize situations and really believe the world hates you and you are always angry. Expect the worst and hope for the best!

Habitual anger has as its core tenet the unwillingness of the person to change their negative, faulty thinking style. They believe they are right to be angry all the time because in many ways they really believe people are purposely out to make them miserable. The greatest challenge of the individual with habitual anger is to try and change their irrational thinking. They literally are the ones who never hope for the best, but always expect the worst. They are pessimistic thinkers who believe that by being guarded in their emotions, that is being cynical all the time, they don't run the risk of being disappointed. Habituated thinkers are lazy thinkers! They never challenge preconceived notions and irrational beliefs.

They take whatever they are given and go with it even though their perceptions are totally wrong. They are the bearers of doom and gloom.

Remember, stereotypes are short cuts to perceptions. When you think according to stereotypes, you are acting as a passive thinker. You are not challenging your thought process to see other reasons, options or outcomes. You are most likely to interpret similar situations the same way. In fact, you may even start using the same reaction for all situations, angry thinking!

In one of the scenarios, I mentioned things that people become angry with; bad weather, waiting in lines, technical inconveniences and other unfortunate situations. Do you get angry when these things happen to you? If you answered yes, then I have this next question for you. How does getting angry possibly help, improve or change the situation? It doesn't! Getting angry over things out of your control only frustrates matters and always makes things worse.

Habituated anger in many ways is like an addiction. This type of anger has already become habit forming for the individual. Remember, some addictions are the by-product of conditioning. When situations arise, something stimulates you and you respond. Over time, we become sensitized or conditioned to respond to situations that are the same. This process leads to habituation, even addiction!

Last year I had a great discussion with Jack Canfield, co-creator of *Chicken Soup For The Soul* and his great new book *The Success Principles For Healthy Habits*. Anyone possessing habituated anger should definitely consider reading his book. Canfield told me habits are useful in that they help people save time, but unfortunately the habits you are currently using are only good enough to get you to where you currently are!

People with habituated anger require changing their habituated thinking patterns and responses. They need to challenge themselves to create new scripts for responding to situations which may look the same or be altogether different. You need to modify lazy thinking patterns!

12

PASSIVE-AGGRESSION

♌

Resentment is an extremely bitter diet, and eventually poisonous. I have no desire to make my own toxins.
Neil Kinnock

Are you an individual who doesn't get mad, you just prefer to get even? Do you appear cool as a cucumber on the outside, but feel like a volcano about to erupt on the inside whenever you get into arguments or disagreements? Do you appear to co-operate with others, but inside you plot and create hidden agendas to sabotage other's plans? Do you purposely go out of your way to spread gossip and insults about others, including family and friends? These are all signs of an individual possessing passive-aggressive anger.

Perhaps the best way to depict an individual possessing this anger is they use it to get what they want, which they are usually unsure of what that is to begin with. Their method of operation involves taking advantage of others. Most times, people using anger in this manner get what they intended only to find out it wasn't really what they wanted. Others, who felt taken advantage of avoid them at all costs because they feel used, betrayed and humiliated.

Individuals with passive-aggressive anger most times behave like hypocrites. They say one thing but do another. They literally talk out of both sides of their mouths. Observers will catch this and over a period of time start to feel very uncomfortable around them. Those observing passive-aggressive individuals don't know what to expect other than the general outcome: I will be exploited in some way, shape or form!

From my own experiences working with this anger type, I have found most individuals possess feelings of inferiority. In fact, I believe some would love to take that leap toward the opposite pole of superiority, but either don't know how too or are afraid of whatever success it might bring them.

There is a famous expression which asserts, "I'd rather attempt something great and fail, than do absolutely nothing and succeed". The second part of that expression basically sums up the thought process for an individual using passive-aggressive anger. They want to go somewhere, but they just don't know where. Furthermore, they are threatened by others getting to their destinations, so they don't want them to get there either! I believe many factors have a lot to do with the development of passive-aggressive anger, which would include jealousy, rejection, experiencing abuse, feeling alienated and not setting positive short-term or long-term goals.

What I have learned from individuals with passive-aggressive anger is that many are mimickers or imitators. They are less likely to step out on their own and take risks. Rather, they will try to be like others, copy others, or in some cases even try to become someone they are not! Two exceptional Hollywood movies portray this. If you've never seen Single White Female or The Talented Mr. Ripley, I strongly recommend them. Obviously they are sensationalized to extremes, but they offer you a taste of what an individual with this anger behaves like and could possibly become.

"*Passive-aggressive*" is thrown around quite loosely in society, most times in accusatory joking manners. A few years ago, it became a "catch phrase". The following are examples which show passive-aggressive anger at work.

👍

Scenario #1

Charles has lived in the United States for ten years. He left Denmark after he and his wife split up. He accused her of leaving him and also has said she has made their two daughters hate him. He has never been back to visit them, nor does he call them. Charles took a job in a factory as a skilled tradesman upon arriving in Pittsburgh. He has worked in the same factory ever since. He has few friends and has always felt like he doesn't fit in, even though he tries. For the last two years he has grown tired of his co-worker's jokes and Danish voice imitations. He doesn't find them funny in the least. He has never told them to stop or that it bothers him. He always smiles and goes with the flow. This day is different. He has had enough! He joins his co-workers at the lunch table and listens to their jokes. In fact, he even encourages them to joke about him more. He glances at his watch and leaves the lunch room ten minutes before lunch is over. He goes back to his work place and gets out his blow torch. He goes to his co-workers work sites and heats their wrenches and pliers until the metal is white hot. By the time his co-workers return, the tools are no longer glowing. Several of the workers grab their tools and start screaming. He finds this amusing. Some of the workers suffer second degree burns. Charles is accused of the offence and eventually confesses. The company cannot terminate him as he has been a proficient employee and he also threatens to go to the Human Rights Commission and lodge harassment and racism charges. The company sends him to an anger management group.

What is the cause of Charles's anger? Feeling inferior and totally frustrated.

What are the precipitating factors? Feeling worthless and degraded. By not addressing others with his concerns, it only leads to further feelings of hopelessness and degradation which eventually leads to his perceived need for "getting even".

<u>Scenario #2</u>

Jack is involved in the film industry. He has made several pitches to production companies in an effort to try and get his work produced. Each time his work has been rejected, he has been invited to submit new proposals. A colleague of Jack's, Paul offers him a chance to work on one of his productions. Jack is invited to the first production meeting and reluctantly accepts. He is invited to provide input in their brainstorming session. The team is very upbeat and full of enthusiasm. Whenever Jack offers his ideas, they are always negative and focus on the impossibilities. Paul is concerned with Jack's attitude as several other members of the team view Jack as a "downer". Paul meets with Jack suggesting this project is probably not a good match for him and maybe he should work on his own ideas. Jack agrees and leaves the project. Jack bad-mouths Paul's project to other friends, saying it will never go anywhere and that it is a waste of time. This is what he tells others as to why he left the project.

What is the cause of Jack's anger? Rejection and repeated failures.

What are the precipitating factors? Frustration and rejection due to an elevated sense of self-worth. Jack is very rigid in his thinking and is not willing to co-operate with others and work as a team. Due to his inability to help others succeed in their endeavors, others will not help him with his own.

<u>Scenario #3</u>

Stan is a 12th grader who is very popular amongst his male peers. He is the star of the high school football team. Stan does whatever it takes to succeed. He has often been accused of using people to get ahead. He has a habit of bad mouthing his friends and others to make himself look better. Recently, he asked Susan out, an attractive, popular girl from *his math class. She has been at the top of the honor roll with her grades and belongs to many of the school's organizations. Susan politely declined the invitation saying she was just too busy with school. After Stan insistently pressed her for the date, she finally told him he wasn't her type. Smitten by the rejection, Stan started telling others Susan was a slut. To save face amongst his peers, he told them he had sex with her and that she was "too easy" for his liking. He insisted he likes good, clean girls and not white trailer trash. The gossip quickly made its cycle throughout the school thus tarnishing Susan's reputation. Susan's parents have sought advice from a lawyer to pursue pressing charges against Stan.*

What is the cause of Stan's anger? Rejection.
What are the precipitating factors? Stan's grandiose sense of self and his perception that he is better than everyone else. Stan also views rejection as a sign of failure and can't deal with failure so he creates situations which demean others to make him feel better.

Passive-aggressive anger produces situations and outcomes of uncertainty, chaos, hurt and misunderstandings.

The way most passive-aggressive people deal with situations is to look at how they can twist a situation to suit them without any regard for the feelings of others. Usually neither party feels good about what has happened. Those with passive-aggressive anger may feel victorious or momentarily satisfied at first, however this feeling eventually wanes and they are left with a feeling of emptiness. Especially, if they have hurt or insulted someone, they are definitely likely to feel lonely or be alone!

Having worked with individuals with passive-aggressive anger, one central trait which most possess is their inability to get what they really want in life. In fact, most really don't know what they really want because they tend to fly by the seat of their pants and let things happen as they may. They don't plan well thought out short- term and long-term goals. I once asked an individual I was counseling with passive-aggressive anger about their lack of goals and their response caught me off guard, "It's hard to create and set well-defined goals when you have no basic working definition of yourself." I asked this client what he meant by this and his answer was even more remarkable, "Most people like myself, who are passive-aggressive are really phonies, we are wannabees!" Wow!

WHAT'S YOUR ANGER TYPE?

Passive-aggressive anger is solely rooted in misperception and deception. Not only does the individual with this type of anger do this unto others, but they also do it to themselves. Perhaps the first step in the process for resolving passive-aggressive anger is for the individual to introspect themselves and take a deep look inward. Obviously, what is making you tick isn't working for the best. You need to know the "why's" and "how's" of your behavior. The greatest obstacle for overcoming this type of anger is to accept you are your own worst enemy. You need to realize your behaviors are based on your current thought processes which are not working. You need to modify them. This can only be done only after you have accomplished two things: Knowing who you are and knowing what you really want! There are great self-help books which help individuals find answers to these questions. I suggest taking the inner journey to find the why's and the how's!

13

MORALISTIC ANGER

✝

Holding on to anger is like grasping a hot coal with the intent of throwing it at someone else; you are the one getting burned.

Buddha

Perhaps the best way to define moralistic anger is intense "self-righteousness"! Moralistic anger is based on rigid and fundamentalist thinking.

If you possess this anger type, you probably perceive situations as:

> *Right versus Wrong*
> *Good versus Evil*
> *Black and White*
> *Good or Bad*
> *All or Nothing*

👍

Almost all perceptions for individuals with this type of anger fall on a polarized continuum. Their perceptions reside at either end of the spectrum, but there is no in between. In fact, everything is either/or with no gray areas. For the individual with moralistic anger, they would perceive anything in the "gray area" or middle as non-committal to forming opinions and decisions. They often times refer to those outside the constraints of their thinking process as either the opposition or fence-sitters!

The cause for moralistic anger can usually be traced back to rigid thinking learned from growing up in families who were highly idealistic or extreme fundamentalists. At an early age, children learned there would be no middle ground. Compromises were out of the question! Everything was always based on the all or nothing principle.

Some of the worst wars and conflicts in the history of humanity were caused by moralistic anger. Think about the Nazi Holocaust and the millions of people who were murdered in the name of a cause. What about the discrimination and racism which exists in the world? Perhaps the two greatest causes of racism are fear and ignorance. The worst part of this is that both are by-products of faulty thinking leading to stereotypes. These stereotypes are created because individuals are unable to think for themselves in "gray" terms. Instead, they accept force-fed beliefs which reside on polarities of black or white thinking. They are extremists in the truest sense!

The hypocrisy of the matter is most wars and disputes are created because of religious beliefs. In fact, most if not all religions practice love and peace. When ideals are threatened, love and peace get tossed out the window and violence is seen as a means to attain peace which already existed in the first place before religion and politics got involved! Wars don't kill, people do! And these people kill because of their moralistic anger.

When I work with clients possessing this type of anger I have noticed a central tenet at the root. Many are highly perfectionist in their thinking believing there is no room for failure. Moreover, to be wrong would indicate their failures and shortcomings. This would further reveal to them they are indeed not perfect. The greatest barrier holding them back from thinking flexibly is their fear. Individuals with moralistic anger fear being wrong. Some may feel if they have to compromise then their way of thinking must be wrong. Remember, these individuals think in terms of polarized thinking where there are only two possible outcomes. They are usually hell-bent in their convictions and any shifts toward the center would be viewed as leading toward the opposite pole which they are against. Therefore, they hold on tooth and nail to their set beliefs and opinions. Compromise is not an option! Any compromise would equate with a perception of being wrong which translates to failure. For the those with moralistic anger, convictions are set in stone and frozen like the ice age!

Read the following scenarios and see how you feel about

them. Do you agree with what is going on? Can you see yourself in any of these situations as the rigid thinker?

👍

Scenario #1

A local church has put together a program to bring greater awareness to their community about the sins of having abortions. They preach that abortion is murder! Any woman having an abortion is guilty of killing her child. They target the medical community and assert that Pro Choice centers promote and advocate abortion. They distribute information in front of these centers to women coming in. Several times the police have been called to break up these peaceful demonstrations which have left people passing by feeling uncomfortable. A doctor in the community who performs abortions is labeled a murderer by the church group. In fact, posters with his picture accusing him of infanticide are being posted around the city. Tired of the harassment he decides to close up his practice and move to another city. Upon hearing this, the group is happy they have run him out of town. Still not satisfied, one of the members decides the doctor is getting away too easy to continue his "killing spree". Days later, the doctor is shot dead. The member claims he did it to save the hundreds who were being murdered by the doctor. At his arraignment, the member claims, "Thou shalt not kill, the doctor was doing this and I stopped a murderer!"

What is the cause of the member's anger? An extreme sense of self-righteousness.
What are the precipitating factors? Rigid and fundamentalist thinking which shaded his own ability to discriminate between what is really right and what is really wrong. Ironically, he committed the very act for which he was accusing the doctor and women having the abortions.

<u>Scenario #2</u>

A police officer races down the highway in an unmarked car. You notice he does not have his sirens on. The cop is doing well over the speed limit. What gives him the right to do this when he is not even in pursuit of anyone? You decide that if he can break the law, then you too have the right to do the *same speed as he is doing. You start to tail him and you do so for a couple of miles. Finally, he switches on his signals and moves into the right lane, slowing down. You pass him. As you continue, he flies up behind you and pulls you over. You are just miffed. He asks for your license and registration. You angrily give it to him and also call him a hypocrite. You threaten to challenge the ticket in court claiming you will bring a complaint against the cop for speeding. When the case does go to court, you find out the cop was discretely tailing a suspect with other police officials. Boy, did you assume wrong!*

What is the cause of the anger in this situation? Feeling stupid after making assumptions without having all the facts. Remember the old saying about why you shouldn't assume? What are the precipitating factors? Possessing feelings of self-righteousness even in the face of breaking the law.

<u>Scenario #3</u>

The government raises tuition for all university students. The costs to attend university are already high to begin with. Several students who are disgruntled with the increased costs *decide to protest what the government is doing. They organize a march in front of the minister's office at the government building to voice their differences. They picket all morning as their numbers grow into the hundreds. Finally, the police are called in to break up the unlawful gathering as it is disrupting traffic and irritating other businesses. The police politely ask everyone to leave or they will be forced to charge violators with trespassing and disturbing the peace. Several of the protestors become belligerent and storm the government building. Those making it inside trash the statues in the foyer and also spray paint the walls. They are charged. Total damage is well over $50,000. The damaged statues were paid for through taxpayer's dollars!*

What is the cause of the rioters' anger? Feeling cheated and exploited by the government.

What are the precipitating factors for their anger? Believing they have the right to defend their self-righteous beliefs and force others to listen. Also, believing the means justifies the ends no matter what they are forced to do as they believe since they were being "exploited", they had the right to retaliate in a manner which they deemed necessary.

I have found people acting on their moralistic anger to be very similar to those with passive aggressive anger. The only difference is they are more intentional and actually want the recognition for what they are doing. Like passive aggressive anger, they act first and then think later. Unlike passive aggressive anger, their intentions started out good, but their emotions got out of control. Unfortunately, it is this latter feature which usually gets them in trouble when angry, especially when they believe they are above the law!

Moralistic anger is good for some individuals when it forces them to take a stand or act when they otherwise wouldn't have. Some people are so passive they constantly get taken advantage of. Others are constantly in neutral waiting for others to do their fighting or dirty work for them. I believe most people are at their strongest and most motivated whenever their ideals are threatened. This is sometimes the kick in the butt they need to get them going.

Perhaps some of the greatest heroes and success stories can trace their motivation to moralistic anger. These individuals, when faced with personal adversity were able to rise to the challenge. They looked conflict right in the eyes and didn't back down. This has been the best selling story for those overcoming hardships due to oppression, wars, exploitation and abuse. They would not allow their personal beliefs to be comprised and they were willing to fight for them, even die for them!

Remember, anger itself is not a bad emotion. It is how you use your anger which makes it good or bad. Moralistic anger when used constructively and productively has the greatest potential for doing good. Some of the greatest historical movements for example; abolishment of slavery, survivors of the Holocaust, Women's Liberation, Christianity and free democracies happened because of moralistic anger. Brave and resilient people believed in a cause and were willing to go the distance. No matter how great the challenges or the threats, these people were willing to stand strong. In fact, they were typically the recipients of aggression but they wouldn't succumb to failure. They weren't fighting because something wrong was done to them and they were seeking vengeance. Instead, they were seeking to do what was right to correct the situation because an enormous insult was done to others as well as themselves.

When moralistic anger is used constructively, closed doors and boarded windows have a way of getting opened. The key to getting what you want through this anger is to know what you want and then address your intentions with others through discussions and compromise. Obviously, the examples I mentioned above included wars where violence unfortunately became the only solution. Even then, it was done for what was best for the greatest good. Your moralistic anger should not be rooted in aggression and violence. If you are propagating peace, then you shouldn't be brandishing a gun to get peace! Moralistic anger is used to correct a "wrong doing" rather than provoking that wrong into greater insults.

It is very hard to rationalize when you are irrational. Moralistic anger is one of those anger types where the rational (proper ideals) can spill into the irrational (improper behaviors). The key to getting what you really want is to use your moralistic anger as a motivating factor to create change, but you do so in an assertive, amicable, and peaceful manner.

14

MANIPULATIVE ANGER

☠

Malice drinks one-half of its own poison.

Seneca

WHAT'S YOUR ANGER TYPE?

Has anyone ever referred to you as a poor sport or a crybaby? When you were a child, when you didn't get your way did you pack up your toys and go home? Did you refuse to play with others who didn't want to play by your rules? Are you a sore loser? Are you any or all of the above today? If you answer yes, then you might have manipulative anger!

What is manipulative anger? It can best be described as scheming or controlling behaviors used to get you what you want. The famous psychiatrist Eric Berne described three states people play; the balanced adult role, the parent role and the child role. The balanced adult role is behaving and acting responsibly. You focus on the here and now. The parent and the child roles can be used in the proper context or in ways which generate dysfunction. For example, a parent plays the parent role through nurturing or caring for their children. On the other hand, a married woman may play the parent role to her irresponsible drug using, alcohol abusing husband. She thus enables his behavior and treats him like a child! An adult male may play the child role when he joins his friends for a game of pickup hockey. Within this situation, the child role is used appropriately. Conversely, this same man might throw a temper tantrum when he learns his wife has made plans to go out as a family the same night he had plans to play hockey. To get even, he sulks and pouts the whole night. This is obviously playing the child role in a dysfunctional manner. Children use anger to manipulate, so do adults!

Most individuals possessing manipulative anger usually show one or both traits of self-centeredness and impatience. Both of these traits were learned in early childhood and continue to thrive into adulthood. The self-centeredness trait usually evolved from parents who spoiled their children and bent over backwards for them. They thought they were being great parents by giving their children everything they asked for. Impatience developed when the child didn't get their own way and threw tantrums until they got what they wanted. Their parents usually gave in to keep peace and shut the kid up! I often wondered who this ploy was geared toward; trying to really make the kid happy, or giving the kid what they wanted so they wouldn't have to listen to them? I am sure most times it was the latter which became habit after enabling the child's response in the first place!

Have you ever been out shopping and observed some child wailing and screaming as if their parent was torturing them in the most heinous way? As you get closer to the screaming child you hear parts of the conversation. You learn the child is crying over the fact their parent refused to buy them the coveted box of cereal they wanted containing the special prize. Their parent decides to apply some quick pop psychology they just learned from some expert telling them its okay to say "no" and just let the child cry. Furthermore, they are told to "just ignore the child" even when they are out in public. "Great", I've always thought to myself. I've watched this "skit" play itself out in the supermarket and I usually observe the same outcome. The child's face starts to turn redder as they scream louder. They eventually plop themselves on the floor and start flopping around like a salmon out of water. People start staring at the parents hoping they will do something. The parents start to grow embarrassed. This facilitates an immediate response to make all parties happy. Into the shopping cart goes the coveted box of cereal. Case closed! The crying stops and the child is instantly relieved. It's like a wonder drug. Fellow grocery shoppers are thankful they don't have to listen to the shrieking, their eardrums are spared further abuse! And best of all, the parent has controlled the situation once again. Or have they? Who controls who? If the parent was in control of the situation, then why not just put the cereal in the basket in the first place and save yourself and others the torment? On the other hand, does the child hold all the cards because they know if they scream long enough they will win?

If I was a betting man, I would put my money down on the child! This is a conditioned response the parent has created. They have taught their child the longer and louder you cry, I will buckle under pressure and give into you. The child already knows this because they have played this broken record, slow dance since they were young enough to recognize how powerful an actor they are in the situation. Basically, the child has the parent trained!

Some of the worst cases I see manipulative anger at play is with couples coming in for marital counseling. After a few moments of counseling, you notice the roles being divided and differentiate the parent from the child. Interestingly, this dysfunctional "parent-child" dichotomy is usually at the root of their marital discord.

Here are a few examples where manipulative anger is at work. Perhaps you can see yourself in these situations behaving like the child?

WHAT'S YOUR ANGER TYPE?

Scenario #1

You live in a dorm at college. You have a roommate. Your desk is on one side of the room and your mate's is on the other. You are listening to soft music as you do your homework. Your mate comes into the room and puts on the television set, quite loud. Rather than ask them to lower it, you turn the volume up on your stereo. Your mate looks at you and smiles. They turn up the volume on the television. Before you know it, you are exchanging volume changes until both of you have the volume cranked up as high as they will go. The neighbors next door are wrapping loud on the walls at the ruckus. You refuse to lower the volume until your roommate turns the volume down on the television. She finally lowers it and shakes her head at you. You nod to her and lower the volume on your stereo. You win! Your roommate gets up to leave and turns to you. "All you had to do was ask and I would have lowered it in the first place", she says.

What is the cause of anger in this situation? Believing you

should be respected and catered too in all situations, even when compromise is an option.

What were the precipitating factors? Possessing a grandiose sense of self and believing you are entitled to anything and everything you want.

Scenario #2

Sam and Jane are a married couple having a discussion about their son. Jane makes a statement to Sam that he is never around and always working. She wishes he would make more time for their son and start attending more of his baseball games and school activities. Sam asserts he is working hard to give both of them a better lifestyle. Jane says she appreciates it, but still wants Sam to try harder and spend more time doing things with their son. Sam becomes miffed by Jane's allegation he is not a good father. Jane tells him she never implied he was a bad father and never insinuated anything of the sort. Jane tries to explain her point and make him understand her intention. Sam's response is "whatever". She continues the conversation and Sam turns up the volume on the television. Insulted, Jane tells Sam she doesn't appreciate his immaturity.

Sam's response is "whatever". Frustrated, she tells him she is going to bed. Sam's response, "whatever".

What is the cause of Sam's anger? Personalizing Jane's constructive criticism as a direct attack on his fathering skills. What are the precipitating factors? It could be that Sam realizes Jane is speaking some truth and feels guilty. Also, it could be that Sam is used to making all the decisions and feeling in control. He can't stand the fact that he is wrong and interprets Jane as being a "mother figure" to him and trying to correct him. Sam definitely has an enflamed ego!

<u>*Scenario #3*</u>

Kim is a 17 year old who just got her driver's license. Her father lets her use the family car, but has placed a 10 p.m. curfew for having the car home. It is Friday night and her friends are planning to go to a dance which is outside of the city limits. None of them drive. Kim is the only driver among them. They ask her if she would be able to drive. This is going to be the dance of the year! Anyone who is part of the "in crowd" will be there. Kim feels the urgency to be a part of this event.

By driving her friends, she will definitely be the cool young lady her friends are painting her out to be. She asks her father for the car and he has no objection other than she is to have it back by 10 p.m. She argues it is not a school night and his demands are ridiculous. He tells her it has to be back by 10 p.m. or no car. She argues with him and makes some unruly remarks. Offended and hurt by her remarks, he revokes the use of the car and also grounds her. Upset by the turn of events, she threatens to run away from home. Her father tells her to do what she feels she should do. She makes further remarks such as, "I'm not kidding, I will run away and you will never see me again." Hurt but appearing not phased by her remarks, he walks away from her. She screams at him, "I hate you!"

What is the cause of Kim's anger? Getting her request rejected when she felt she is entitled to anything she wants.
What are the precipitating factors? Perhaps Kim has gotten too much in the past and is used to stretching the limits with her father and this time he is making no compromise. She may be used to using power plays such as threats to get her way and this time it is not working and this enrages her.

Manipulative anger can perhaps best be described as a form of regression. The individual regresses into a thinking state which is based on, "me, me, me". Early on they learned that if they pouted or carried on like a spoiled brat, their parent would give in. In fact, parents unconsciously reward their behaviors and only encourage them to continue behaving this way.

There is an old saying, "if it isn't broken, don't fix it". Well, for the individual using their manipulative anger to get what they want, they don't view their behavior as needing to be fixed. Furthermore, even if you are aware the behavior you are using is inappropriate but it is getting you everything you want, do you think you will be inclined to want to change it? Remember, any change on your part is going to take work and that might require too much thought and energy. On the other hand, you may keep "winning" and getting what you want at the risk of pushing family, friends and people away from you. Over time, people will become tired of your spoiled sport antics. If people keep telling you to grow up they might really mean change your selfish behavior and be more co-operative.

People grow frustrated when others behave like children. Adults will say they are ready to pull their hair out because of their child's immature behavior. Just think how much more frustrating it is to deal with adults acting the same way? I find people who keep behaving this way eventually wind up alone as no one wants to parent or mentor them because most choose to remain the same.

Manipulative anger is often a short cut for conflict resolution, which involves honest and mature communication. Communication takes work with the investment of ideas and feelings. Those using manipulative anger are lazy when it comes to resolving conflicts. They take shortcuts toward a dysfunctional resolution. They only want what they want and what is best for them. They really don't care about the other person's feelings when the conflict is occurring. In fact, these individuals tend to be conflict avoidant of situations which reveal their own short-comings and mistakes. Their arguing and childlike behaviors become a power play to detract from the real issues. I have found their pouting and sulking are smoke screens to try and make the other individual feel guilty and cave in. For those dealing with individuals using manipulative anger, if you refuse to cave in, then they would have to re-evaluate their problem solving skills and change them. Stop enabling them to behave as children and encourage them to modify their dysfunctional thinking patterns. Some experts might refer to this as "tough love" which is often used by parents with their teenagers. Tough love is based on the ability to say one word and mean it: NO! Most parents are afraid their teens will hate them or they will push them away. Well, the opposite is actually true. Teens will learn to respect their parent's answers and learn others will always hold more power in certain situations. The same is true for those using manipulative anger. Tough love is never out of vogue for any age or gender. By saying no and not giving in, you are telling others you care because you are truly doing what is best for them. Moreover, you are telling them you no longer think of them as a child. You are an adult and you are going to treat adults like adults should be treated!

15

WHAT MOTIVATES YOUR ANGER?

If you do not wish to be prone to anger, do not feed the habit, give it nothing which may tend to its increase.

Epictetus

WHAT MOTIVATES YOUR ANGER?

In the lectures I teach on addictions, I cover motivation and motivational interviewing. Since people with anger management problems posses anger in much the same way an addict possess and acts out an addiction, I thought I would break it down even further into motivating factors.

Did you know there are only 2 things which motivate people? Gain and fear! In fact, if you are motivated by extremes of gain, then you would be said to be motivated by personal greed.

I want you to take a few moments and make a list of things you believe you are motivated by. These could be people in your life, things that you own or hope to own, activities you do, places you spend time at, your biggest turn-ons or things you most try to avoid.

Anything which drives you to want more, or you stand to accumulate personal profit on would fit under the heading of gain. Anything you try to avoid because it produces any amount of anxiety or fear would fit under fear. Everything on your list will fall under one of these two headings. I sometimes get people asking me, well what about religion? People will assert religion, moreover faith doesn't fit under either category. They believe it is its own entity. Wrong! If I am a Christian and believe in my faith, I do so because I want to walk through those pearly gates. Conversely, by being a Christian, my faith and salvation will keep from going to the less desirable destination called hell! What's even more interesting, is that once people recognize religion falls under motivational reasoning, they can further introspect and determine why they are religious in the first place. Do you subscribe to your faith for reasons of fear, or are you religious because you believe you will gain something? Not to turn this into a religious book, but I will point out that when people's religious convictions are strongly motivated by fear, they are more likely to possess moralistic anger! I have found that religious fundamentalism is largely based in fear and this can lead to very irrational, egotistical beliefs thus spurning their anger.

I want you to look at your list of motivating factors. I now want you to place them under one of three columns.

WHAT'S YOUR ANGER TYPE?

Motivated By Gain	*Motivated By Fear*	*Motivated By Gain/Fear*
1.	1.	1.
2.	2.	2.
3.	3.	3.
4.	4.	4.
5.	5.	5.

Now that you have that done, I want you to look first at the "Motivated By Gain" column. Is there anything in your list which suggests that greed has developed? I am a firm believer people should definitely strive for what they really want in their lives. There is definitely nothing wrong with being successful and gaining more. When does striving for success become a bad habit, even a bad addiction? When your life falls out of balance and you are basically becoming a workaholic because of greed. You are no longer functioning optimally. Instead you have an "addiction to work" for all the wrong reasons. In essence, your passion for what you love doing gets driven by greed.

Gain is a great motivator because it helps us achieve both short-term and long-term goals. Without goals we would be living with one foot in the grave. Goals give people reasons to live and want to get out of bed every morning. Most people I have met who lack goals are very miserable because they tend to be lost. They possess no direction. In fact, those lacking direction because they lack goals are people most likely to possess resistant anger and jealousy! If you possess these types of angers, could the reason be your lack of goal setting?

Gain is good. Goals are great! By focusing on both of these things in your life it leaves you little time to commiserate and be miserable. Goals keep you in cruise control, preventing you from getting hung up by road blocks or racing against time recklessly!

It is when your sense of gain becomes enflamed and swells into "greed" that anger management problems are most likely to occur. People motivated by greed are likely to find their lives spinning out of control. It is like hitting a patch of black ice at high speed and not being able to regain control of your car. Most individuals who get caught in their own world of greed begin developing perfectionist personalities. The bottom line, everything becomes all or nothing for you. The only thing you will accept for yourself is success. You begin placing unrealistic expectations on yourself. You become a perfectionist!

Whenever you place unrealistic expectations on yourself you definitely set yourself up for a world of frustration and failure. Perfectionists possess words like "must" and "should" which leads them no room for compromise. Anything short of what they want to attain would mean they have failed. The longer most people operate under the premise of greed, the more likely they are to operate outside the box of principles and morals they had hoped to live by.

Have you ever met someone or heard about someone who changed because they became rich or started earning a lot of money? It's as if this person changed over night! You'd swear aliens abducted them and robbed them of their integrity. The more money some people possess, the more they become misers! Money does not buy happiness for most people. Instead, they become more miserable. Some are driven for more not because of their greed for becoming richer, but their fear of believing they do not possess enough! This is also greed.

Greed usually has at its behavioral roots aggression. Aggression is getting what you want at whatever cost. Aggression knows not empathy or sympathy. People who get in your way are steamrolled over. They are viewed more as obstacles and nuisances. Since they are viewed as obstacles, you are more likely to disregard their needs and desires. The more they frustrate you in attaining your greed-based goals, the more likely you are to act out aggressively toward them. In fact, your perception of people as obstacles to your success could facilitate hostilities or even a hatred of others. You might grow very angry and miserable around others. Your primary response becomes one of anger. Ever watched the movie "A Christmas Carol"? What do you think Scrooge was made of? He was definitely a man cut from the cloth of greed!

Greed has a way of leading people to act without empathy. To be empathetic is to put yourself in another's shoes and see why it is they are doing what they are doing, feeling what they are feeling, and truly trying to understand them. Greed does not allow for this experience of interpretation. All empathy is over-ruled by the individual's lust for greater success and acquisitions. Individuals who are around "greedy" individuals will pick up on their selfishness and start avoiding them. I have seen so many who have the most money, houses, cars and material possessions who are the loneliest. They may never truly be alone, however deep down they are very lonely. They strive to attain more hoping this will remove their feelings of loneliness. Unfortunately, this is rarely the case!

I have found working with some people who have the most and who want more (the greedy types) are usually the unhappiest. They will tell me they dislike people because people only use them or want something from them. They have developed trust issues. They can't discern between who is authentic versus who is out to bilk them. So rather than take a chance trusting again, they choose to remain alone and miserable. After years of feeling alone and miserable, they want to know how they can be happy again! Furthermore, many of them possess "anger issues" as they call it and want to know how to overcome their hostile feelings.

I have found that most people with trust issues are this way due in part because they don't trust their own judgment. Greed has blinded them and literally robbed them not only in their ability to be empathetic to others, but to themselves as well. They have become so displaced from their own feelings they have severed ties from getting in touch with themselves. They doubt their own decision making skills which leads to frustration and disappointment. These recurring experiences lead to stress which eventually creates misery. This misery becomes habitual anger which the individual has a hard time shaking. Eventually, not only are they greedy and miserable, but now they have anger management issues.

A book I highly recommend reading is *Cracking The Millionaire Code* written by Mark Victor Hansen, co-creator of *Chicken Soup For The Soul* and Robert G. Allen. I spoke to Hansen and asked him his views on greed versus financial success. He believes greed is never solved. His advice is to tithe and give as this truly gets people excited and makes them happy!

Fear too is a very terrible motivator. Fear leads most individual to act out in random and unplanned ways. Fear acted upon is usually a knee jerk reaction. I am sure there are situations when people need to act out of fear for survival, such as tragic situations or when lives are threatened. These are heat of the moment situations where immediate action is called for. Even then, looking back on these situations, most people will say they handled the matter as best as they could given what they had, but wish they could have had more time to plan.

When I refer to fear as a motivator, I am asserting fear as the prime and only motivating factor for the individual in all situations. They go to work because they fear losing their job. They get married because they are afraid of being alone. They have children because they fear their biological clock is ticking. They don't take chances or risks because they are afraid of failure. They settle for mediocrity because they might lose everything they have. They believe it is better to hold on to what they have and not lose it, than strive for more and take a chance for something better. They literally always stay in the shallowest of ends because they are afraid of drowning. The funny part is they may even know how to swim or could learn how to swim but their fear immobilizes them!

The contradiction about living in fear is people believe this is what is most comforting and safest. They hold on tooth and nail to what they've got! The thought of taking any kind of risk or chance is discomforting. Conversely, those with fear as their prime motivator tend to resent the success of others who have taken risks. Here some well-known comments, maybe you've heard some of them or used them yourself:

"It's just a matter of time before his luck is going to run out."
"Life is not fair!"
"Some people get all the breaks!"
"I was dealt a bad hand."
"It's just a matter of time before lady luck shines on me."

"People who play the stock market or speculate are no different from gamblers."

"We're going to pay for this later!"

"What goes around comes around."

"Everything always evens up."

"I'm safest behind my four walls."

"Hope for the best, but expect the worst."

"You can't fail if you don't try."

"I'd rather keep what I have than take risks to have more."

"If it's meant to be..."

"No harm no foul."

"I don't believe in taking chances."

"I believe I am middle of the road."

"I like things plain and simple."

👍

Imagine living your life this way? What do you actually have to look forward too, growing old and dying? This way of thinking is horrible, not to mention depressing! In being motivated by fear, you create a sense of learned helplessness for yourself. You surrender living and just exist.

WHAT'S YOUR ANGER TYPE?

Jealousy was one of the types of anger I discussed earlier. Jealousy is perhaps the most common anger type motivated by fear. People living ultraconservative lives whine and complain about others who are more successful than they are. They ask, "why them and not me?" My question to this type of thinking is, why not them? Perhaps they took the chances you were too afraid to take! Don't be jealous of other's success because you were too damn lazy to get into the game and answer the call.

Fear as a motivator is usually learned from parents and families. Rather than challenging you irrational fears or lack of assertiveness, you blindly accept things as they are and how things have always been. It is sad because your goals fall well short of your ultimate potential. In fact, some of the goals you set for yourself were predetermined from how your parents lived their own lives, ultraconservative. The latter part of the famous quotation, "I'd rather attempt to do something great and fail, than do absolutely nothing and succeed" becomes your unconscious mission statement. Is it any wonder why you are always unhappy and miserable? You are your own worst enemy. You resent the success and perseverance of others because you are unwilling to step out of the windowless boxes you live in and take chances. Many times when you try to step out of the box, your conditioned apprehension incapacitates you. This frustrates you. You get angry at yourself and of course others, who are willing to take chances. I've been asked before, "what advice would you give to someone living this way?" My advice is simple and honest. "Just do it damn it and live!" Try life!

16

ANGRY PERSONALITIES

Anger dwells only in the bosom of fools.
        Albert Einstein

PERSONALITY TYPES

Every individual has a unique and different personality. Some people are extroverted. They are emotionally expressive. They like to talk and socialize. They like to engage in a multitude of activities. They are the life of the party. They wear their hearts on their sleeves. Others might be introverted. They keep to themselves. They don't like displaying their emotions. They keep everything inside. They avoid social situations and people. They prefer their own company over the company of others. These two personality types are obviously extremes.

INTROVERTED X-------x-----x--------x--------x--------x-------X EXTROVERTED
(withdrawn/quiet)   *(outgoing/expressive)*

Most people usually fall somewhere in the middle between the large "X's". If you are living in the western world, which is highly competitive and requires people to be more outgoing, being totally introverted probably won't get you what you want. On the other hand, being excessively extroverted could also produce drawbacks as you might be accused of being too aggressive and obnoxious. This is why falling in between and practicing some degree of moderation management for emotions is perhaps the optimal way to be.

INTROVERTS VERSUS EXTROVERTS

How do you perceive the words "Introverted" and "Extroverted"? Do you have positive connotations with one or both words? Do you view one as being more negative than the other? Since this book is about anger and anger management, let's look at some of the nuances with each of these styles when they apply to anger.

Firstly, there is nothing wrong with either one of these personality styles. Extremes of these styles may fit some people like a glove and totally work for them. Others on the other hand may feel totally uncomfortable trying to act introverted or extroverted when this is not the makeup of their personalities. Much like anger, it is how you express it or use it which determines whether it is an asset or liability!

What types of anger do you think fit in with *Introverted* personality style? Remember, introverts tend to keep things inside and have a hard time expressing or asserting themselves. Reread through the various anger types. From clients I have worked with possessing introverted personalities, I have found the following anger styles matching up with this personality style:

> RESISTENT/PASSIVE ANGER
> JEALOUSY ANGER
> PASSIVE-AGGRESSION ANGER
> MANIPULATIVE ANGER
> INTERNET/COMPUTER ANGER

👍

All of these anger types have one thing in common; the inability to express feelings in a mature, honest, assertive manner. Almost everything gets locked up inside and stays inside. Perhaps if the introverted individual with these types of anger management problems was to slide along the personality scale toward extroversion, they might find precipitators of their anger dramatically change. Of course this is going to take time and effort. I highly recommend self-esteem/assertiveness classes, seminars and reading self-help books.

What about an *Extroverted* personality style? What types of anger do you think fall within its domain? Here is what I came up based on the observations and reports of my clients:

ADDICTIVE ANGER
COMPRESSIVE ANGER
ROAD RAGE
CONFLICTUAL ANGER
HABITUATED ANGER
MORALISTIC ANGER

👍

Since extroverts are more emotionally ardent, their anger types would definitely reflect their personalities. People who are extremely passionate about life also tend to be passionate when expressing their emotions. Some emotions expressed too passionately can be very discomforting for others. Anger is definitely one of these emotions. Extreme extroverts with anger management problems might take anger management classes and workshops which would teach them how to become more assertive when expressing anger. There are so many great books on this subject.

Most individuals do not really take the time nor do they care to learn about themselves and their personality styles. Hey, if it works and it isn't broken, then why fix it, right? For those wanting to learn more about themselves and their personality styles, there are courses offered at colleges and universities which are definitely worth taking. Also, there are exceptional, non-clinical books worth reading. I have a list of books I would highly recommend for those interested in learning more about personalities.

(See Recommended Reading List Appendices).

BEHAVIORAL STYLES

Some psychologists and learning theorists would assert that personalities are set by the time we reach adolescence. Some believe who we are then is who we will always be. Our personalities define who we are and what we are. I agree with these theories to an extent. I do believe we can modify or intensify our personalities through our behaviors. Behaviors are always being learned, reshaped and modified throughout our lives. They are never set in stone unless we want them to be. We can change them. We can unlearn negative behaviors we don't want or like! Just like dogs, we are never too old to be taught new tricks!

There is an analogy I use with clients and students when discussing the difference between personality style and behavior. If you own a DVD player, I want you to imagine that is your personality. It is the hardware which plays movies. It remains the same unless you adjust the control switches on it. It can and will play only the DVD's you insert into it. Correct? Well, let's say for the most part you are a movie buff like me. You watch lots of movies. You are always looking for something good to watch which will entertain you. You watch your movie to escape from the real world for a couple of hours. The movie ends and you remove it from the player. The DVD player remains in a state of flux until you load the next movie. Are you with me so far?

Now let's say you pick up a new release from the video store. It's movie night and you are excited about the prospect of being entertained for a couple of hours. You load the movie. You've got your popcorn ready to eat and the movie begins.

WHAT'S YOUR ANGER TYPE?

Twenty minutes into the movie you realize you've picked a dud! The movie really sucks! You are very disappointed and decide not to watch the rest of it. At this point what do you do? Do you bring the DVD back to the store? Or, do you bring your DVD player to the store and complain that it plays bad movies? I am sure some people have done the latter! Rather, you would bring the DVD back since it is not the DVD player's fault that the movie you picked tanked! In fact, if you purchased the movie and possess compressive anger, you might actually drill the movie at the wall! Hopefully, you wouldn't throw the DVD player at the wall or else that would be a very expensive lesson!

The point I am trying to make is you don't throw out the baby with the bath water! The DVD player is like the personality and the DVD's are in essence the behaviors the personality plays. Knowing this, you could have a less desirable personality capable of being adjusted through the modification of your behaviors. All hope is not lost!

If you want to play good movies in the DVD player, it is a good idea to read up on the movie to learn about what you are watching. If you want to act out good behaviors, then it is an even better idea to learn about the various behavioral styles you can use.

There are a multitude of behaviors people engage in on a daily basis. Most behaviors are acted out to suit the personality style of the individual, or they are held onto because some people are too lazy to change them. You always have the ability to think what you want to think and act how you want to act. With that said, you can modify or change any behavior you are uncomfortable with.

For the purpose of this chapter, I am going to break behaviors down into 5 distinct categories:

- *ASSERTIVE*
- *AGGRESSIVE*
- *EXPLOSIVE*
- *PASSIVE-AGGRESSIVE*
- *PASSIVE*

I will explain how these behaviors differ from one another and are unique in their own right. As I asserted earlier, you can modify or change any behavior.

ASSERTIVE BEHAVIORS

Assertiveness is the hallmark of success in personal and professional living. People who are assertive go places in life. In fact, they get to where they want to go and further. The greatest reason for their success is their ability to behave assertively. Moreover, their assertiveness breeds the element most important to personal success: RESPECT!

People behaving assertively give and get respect from others. They understand that in order for their own success to occur, it is beneficial to help others reach their goals. Assertive people understand empathy and how it works. Simply defined, empathy is the ability to put yourself in another person's shoes and see the world through their eyes. You are able to relate to what they are thinking and feeling. If you are able to relate to their personalities, then you are more likely to understand them. If you are taking the time to understand someone, then it shows them you care and respect them. Respect is the key element to assertiveness!

To be assertive is to be goal oriented. You set both short-term and long-term goals. When you set goals, you set targeted destinations for yourself. You are in motion moving toward something desired. This is the first part of assertiveness, knowing what you want. The second part of the assertiveness equation is going out and getting it. What becomes more important is not going out and getting it, rather how you go out and get it. Assertive people get things by respecting others as well as themselves. Assertive people are driven. Yes they are motivated by gain. And they rarely settle for mediocrity. They want more in life!

Perhaps one of the greatest books ever written on assertiveness which has become a landmark bestseller for decades is *How To Win Friends And Influence People* written by Dale Carnegie. The key premise of Carnegie's book is developing exceptional communication skills based on assertiveness training. I highly recommend reading this book or taking one of the many Carnegie courses offered around the world.

Assertive people understand that others have feelings too. They understand the human factor. They learn not to walk over others to get what they want. They understand that lying and cheating is wrong. They reject the manipulation and exploitation of others. Aggression and violence is not part of their problem solving make-up. They understand that open and honest communication is the best standard. Sometimes others might not like hearing what you have to say, however you gain their respect due to your honesty. Assertive people separate the person from their actions. If someone does something wrong or bad, you bring it to their attention. You criticize the behavior and not the individual. Remember, you don't throw the baby out with the bath water! The assertive person separates the artist from their work so to speak. If they recognize someone is doing something wrong, they constructively criticize to help the other person get it right. They realize that most if not all situations are "win-win". If you help someone change their behavior for the better, it will also make your situation better. Assertive people realize this.

Assertive individuals do not practice short cuts to perceptions more commonly known as stereotypes. They are fact finders and truth seekers. They use their communication skills to learn about others. They pay attention to details and try to remain objective. They focus on educating themselves from their experiences to make themselves wiser. Truly successful, assertive people believe there are no failures, rather lessons learned through living. When applying these principles to their daily living, others hold them in high esteem.

Others want to be around you when you are assertive. They trust your judgments. They view you as rational and objective. Have you ever had someone come to you with a problem and they sought your advice? If you were overly critical and emotional with them, they probably grew apprehensive in coming to you with future problems. No one wants to get ripped apart and criticized, right? Assertive people realize this and they are problem solvers. Their minds operate from a solution-focused perspective. They believe every problem possesses within it solutions and they want to find them. If you are overly emotional, your feelings will blind you causing you to miss possible solutions.

Do you know anyone who flies off the handle whenever you bring your problems to them? I am guessing by now you avoid telling them your problems, right? On the other hand, I am sure friends and colleagues who are caring listeners enjoy both your trust and respect.

When it comes to anger, assertive people just get mad, they don't get even. They don't make impetuous decisions in the heat of the moment. They know when to take time outs to ground their emotions. They are truly the "grace under fire" people. They acknowledge their anger and then know when to let go of it. They know how to stop their anger from running and ruining them. They recognize anger as a normal part of their lives as they do other emotions. Assertive people know where to draw the line in all facets of their lives, including how they experience anger.

AGGRESSIVE BEHAVIORS

An aggressive behavioral style is what it sounds like, behavior rooted in aggression. Many people assume that aggression is the same as violence and that is not always true. You can behave aggressively but never become violent. On the other hand, when you become violent you are always aggressive, that is exceedingly aggressive!

What is an aggressive behavioral style? In many ways it looks like assertiveness at many levels until you remove the empathetic component. Remember, empathy is taking into account the other person's feelings and needs. Empathy is non-existent in aggressive behavior. Aggressive individuals choose to become ignorant to the feelings of others. Aggressive behavior is best described as getting what you want without recognizing or acknowledging the needs of others. Simply put, it's steamrolling over others to get what you want!

Working with clients in anger management groups, classes and one on one for years has taught me most individuals with aggressive personality styles suffer from "me first" syndrome. Whether they actually say it or imply it, you can't miss their resounding, "me, me, me". It is almost like a tenor warming up for a coveted solo.

People with aggressive personality styles most often seek out people with weaker personalities to dominate. Their prime candidate is someone with a passive behavioral style who will put up with their abuse! Assertive people recognize aggressive individuals and avoid them, or minimize their involvement with them. Assertive people seek out amicable, "win-win" situations. They recognize that aggressive individuals play for keeps. Aggressive individuals never play to lose.

People with aggressive personality styles play to win. You will often hear them refer to people in general as "winners" and "losers". They are polarized thinkers, where winners versus losers are on the extreme ends of their continuum. Assertive people recognize the gray areas between the poles and hope to bring people around them toward the "winner's" pole. Aggressive people don't care about losers as long as they win and get what they want! In fact, many aggressive people take comfort in seeing others lose as it makes them feel more powerful!

Perhaps one of the most telling qualities of people with aggressive behavior is most times they act before thinking. Moreover, they may think but their thinking doesn't encompass all potential consequences as they are hell-bent on getting their own way. Aggressive people do not consider the feelings of others. When aggressive people are angry their emotions rule. They fly by the seat of their pants! Instead of stepping back and collecting their thoughts, they use their anger as a "super charger" to drive them even more.

Aggressive people are individuals who need to step back from situations where their emotions flood their ability to remain rational. In essence, they need to take time outs! Several anger types match up with aggressive behavior. Perhaps the most common types identified are:

- *Compressive Anger*
- *Addictive Anger*

- *Jealousy*
- *Road Rage*
- *Conflictual Anger*
- *Moralistic Anger*

Bare in mind any of the anger types listed in this book could be identified as fitting into any of the behavioral styles, but you tend to find specific types fitting like a glove with certain personalities.

If you ever have a chance to read any books on stress or personality types, check out type A and type B personalities. Extreme type A personalities fit quite nicely with aggressive behavioral styles. Extreme type A's are people who are highly aggressive and driven by success. They possess several qualities which make their aggressiveness more pronounced. They are more likely to be hostile. They get what they want when they want it! They are extremely competitive. Everything becomes a score card for wins and losses. Of course they prefer to be in the winner's circle. Their motto could best be described as, "take no prisoners!" Extreme type A's are also very time urgent and time restricted. Everything is scheduled to the minute or the second. Lateness or unplanned delays send them over the edge. Type A's will resort to extreme means of aggression to succeed. When sudden death overtime crosses them, the rule book gets thrown out and anything goes! I will discuss extreme type B's in the section on Passive Behaviors.

    People behaving aggressively usually will experience some degree of success. Many of them compromise friendships, partnerships and working relationships at the expense of their desire for success. Do you like being ordered around or bossed around? Do you like working for someone who is very successful, but likes to yell, scream and belittle employees? Do you like to feel like you need to walk on egg shells around certain people because they might get "mad" at you? This is what it is like being around aggressive people. Most people are too afraid to confront the aggressive individual because they are afraid they might get chastised. Furthermore, those having the guts to confront the aggressive individual will usually find their constructive criticisms are met with resistance, disbelief and accusations of jealousy, insecurity or stupidity! Remember, the true essence of the aggressive individual is to get what they want and not care about others, or what others think and feel. Aggressive types become their own worst enemy since they push away those who really care. People eventually grow sick and tired of being belittled. People grow weary of being taken for granted. No one likes to be treated like a doormat! Highly success people who are aggressive types usually have clones around them who want to be successful like them and ride their coat tails. When the harsh reality of isolation sets in, they ask themselves "why doesn't anyone like me or care about me?" That's because you pushed them away!

EXPLOSIVE BEHAVIORS

Explosive behavior is very similar to aggressive behavior accept you add a couple of sticks of dynamite, gasoline and matches! People who are over-anxious and quick to react at all times possess explosive behaviors. They are always a spark away from maniacal frenzy!

I have spoken with colleagues of mine who are doctors. On many occasion they have asserted explosive behavioral types are those who are high risk cardiac patients. They tend to always have elevated high blood pressure (non-essential hypertension) which has no clear biological cause. In fact, it is angry thoughts which gets the blood boiling. You can see the veins in their neck or temple pulsating.

Like aggressive behavior types, Explosives are definitely extreme type A personalities. They get what they want, when they want it, how they want it at whatever cost. They do not care who gets in their way. If people get hurt, they view them as "casualties of war". Explosives show no signs of guilt, remorse or shame in doing what they do. If you have a chance to read any abnormal psychology textbooks or The Diagnostic and Statistical Manual IV, do check out the section on Personality Disorders on Axis-II. Pay attention to two specific personality disorders: Anti-social and Borderline. I am not saying all people with explosive behaviors possess these personality disorders, but I will bet most individuals with either of these 2 personality disorders possess explosive behavior styles.

People with explosive behavioral styles possess few, if any close friends. They have associates and colleagues. These people usually associate with them because they have something to gain by being around them. Most people are too afraid to be in their company. They probably have witnessed episodes of extreme aggression or violence and worry they will turn on them. Moreover, some people are just too embarrassed to be around them because of their spur of the moment tirades!

Some of the anger styles which are often seen in explosive behavioral types are as follows:

- *Compressed Anger*
- *Petrified Anger*
- *Addictive Anger*
- *Habituated Anger*
- *Road Rage*
- *Conflictual Anger*

Of all the behavioral styles discussed, Explosives need to learn behavioral management strategies which teaches them assertiveness training. For all the explosive behavioral types of clients I have worked with, the first thing I have taught them is how and when to use "time outs". Just like a parent has to monitor their child's behavior when they are misbehaving, these individuals need to parent themselves! They need to learn how and when to step back. They need to learn to teach themselves when enough is enough! Unfortunately, most individuals who behave this way are very reluctant to seek help and make changes. From my own experiences, as well as other professionals I work with, they only seek help when they are mandated by courts or when they believe this is their last chance to save their marriages or jobs. Most times they seek help for the wrong reasons as they are forced to get help. Furthermore, they are usually looking for a quick makeshift solution to save their bacon. They come in for counseling to change for others. They receive counseling to make the courts and attorneys happy. They seek counseling to learn ways to sweet talk spouses, family members, bosses and co-workers. Rarely do they ever seek change because they believe they need it.

      People with explosive behavioral styles are a lot like alcoholics. They need to lose everything and hit rock bottom before they seek help. I truly believe if they are sincere about changing, anything is possible!

PASSIVE-AGGRESSIVE BEHAVIORS

People who behave passive-aggressively behave much like the passive-aggressive anger style. Often times I've been asked what the ultimate motive or goal is for the passive-aggressive individual? This is tough to answer but I would assert the goal would fall somewhere between the aggressive and the passive behavioral style. Passive-aggressive people get what they think they want, but are rarely sure of what they really want. Their desires are very much like an ice cream parlor's flavor of the month special. They change from moment to moment, thoughts and ideas blow like the wind constantly shifting directions. The funny part is they are unsure of what they really want and those around them are usually at a total loss for what passive-aggressive people want.

Passive-aggressive individuals resemble people with aggressive behavioral styles in the way which they pursue what they want. They too walk over others to satisfy their needs and desires. Furthermore, they are more likely to use and manipulate others to get what they want. In the beginning, others might not be aware they are being used. When they do catch on, passive-aggressive people possess few if any close friends. No one trusts them!

Have you ever been used by someone? Were you able to ever trust that person again or respect them the same way you originally did? Probably not! People are smart and eventually get tired of being played. Passive-aggressive people will try the same shtick, but others start to grow weary and jaded. Passive-aggressive people are always learning new and alternative ways to manipulate others. In the end, passive-aggressive individuals usually find each other. Ironically, they become critical and leery of each other which in some way fashions poetic justice!

Some of the anger types associated with passive-aggressive behaviors fit under the following for obvious reasons:

- *Passive-Aggression*
- *Moralistic Anger*
- *Manipulative Anger*
- *Conflictual Anger*

Aggressive people are quite straightforward when it

comes to expressing emotions. They say what they intend to say. Passive individuals say little or nothing. Passive-aggressive people are an enigma! You rarely ever know where you stand with them. Rarely, do you ever feel comfortable around them. If you are passive-aggressive, you probably feel uncomfortable living in your own skin.

I have worked with many individuals possessing passive-aggression. Those admitting they had a problem were those who introspected long, hard and deep within themselves. What most of them reported is they hated to make decisions and take positions in their lives. Some reported they were forced to make major or serious decisions early in life which led them to grow uncomfortable when taking sides. Some said their inability to make decisions spilled over into other facets of their lives which made them proverbial fence-sitters. Those seeking help to modify or change their passive-aggressive behavioral styles claimed they grew tired of the splinters in their ass. They wanted change! They wanted people to like them and understand them. First, they needed to understand themselves!

Many individuals with personality disorders have at the core of their disorder passive-aggression. I don't know if one manufactures the other as much as it compliments it.

Ironically, it is their narcissism and perfectionism which prevents them from seeking help.

The key element for change for passive-aggressive people is to enhance their decision making skills. Once they master their ability to make decisions for themselves, soundly and rationally, their manipulative, standoffish manners are greatly reduced. They no longer carry the hidden agendas they are accustomed too. Furthermore, they no longer feel the need to use and manipulate others. They learn how to say what they mean. Their goals are defined and everyone involved with them is aware of what they are seeking. They are able to attract people to them and keep people interested in them. They are no longer perceived as threats!

PASSIVE BEHAVIORS

Passive behavior is very similar to passive anger. Both are extremely flaccid! Passive behavioral styles can best be summed up as never getting what you want unless you like wallowing in misery. Passive individuals tend to always get used because they allow others to rob them of their rights. They get mad at others for using them and mad at themselves for allowing themselves to be used!

Passive individuals never seem to get what they want. Unlike passive-aggressive people who are uncertain about what they really want, passive people know what they want but are afraid to go out and get it. In fact, they allow others, likely aggressive individuals to use them and control them. Passive individuals whine about how unfair life is. They allege to be victims. The sad part is they like to play the victim role because it gives them something to complain about!

Some of the most common anger types associated with passive behavior are:

- Resistant/Passive Anger
- Internet/Computer Rage
- Jealousy
- Petrified Anger

The most common element associated with passive individuals is their sense of learned helplessness. They truly believe they are in situations beyond their control. Moreover, they believe they are forced to stay there. Some like to play the martyr's role whereby they allow others to enable their passivity.

Recall aggressive individuals are most likely to possess extreme type A personalities. The opposite is true for passive individuals. They are most likely to possess extreme type B personalities.

Type B personalities are most likely to possess attributes opposite of type A styles. Most type B personalities are very carefree. They get exploited and used by others. Some recognize it, while others are totally oblivious to the fact! Extreme type B's rarely budget their time well. They may wait to the last minute or run out of time because their time management is not very good. They get frustrated because they procrastinate and then when things are due they get flustered by other's expectations. Some Type B's let others use their time so they literally have no time for themselves. They are then likely to complain that no one respects their time! Type B's are non-competitive and are more likely to miss out on things they want. They may even refer to themselves as losers and laugh about it. The sad part is, deep down many really do feel like losers and reduce themselves to this unconscious association.

Much like aggressive behavioral styles, passive individuals require courses, workshops and books on assertiveness training and esteem building. Most are no where near getting what they really want. I have never met an individual robbed of their integrity and dignity who is truly happy. Furthermore, anyone relinquishing their personal freedoms and liberties with the sole purpose of pleasing others is not likely to feel satisfied.

Most passive individuals discuss change, but rarely ever follow through. Like aggressive individuals, they usually have to experience some major life event, tragedy or adversity which will motivate them toward change. So many passive individuals are afraid of change. They dread the potential failure which may ensue through re-creating themselves. Many have known repeated failure and can't imagine the thought of experiencing new kinds of failure. They would rather dance with the devil they know than waltz with the monsters in the light.

Working with passive clients has taught me some people actually find solace and comfort in misery. This feeling becomes akin to them and they choose to hold on to what is known versus the unknown. I once worked with an individual suffering from chronic depression. He offered something very profound,

"The only feeling I have ever known is depression. How would I ever recognize what joy is? And if I did and it was as good as people say, would it not make me more depressed if the joy was suddenly taken away from me? For this very reason, I would rather remain depressed!"

👍

As this outlook probably makes sense to the individual with depression, I am sure it also matches many passive individuals. Passive individuals feel extremely helpless or believe others control them. Even though most are aware they do little to get out of their perceived "hopeless, helpless and hapless" situations, they are content to play the victim role as it gives them masochistic mastery over their lives. This is their sense of control.

I have spoken with colleagues of mine who are medical doctors, psychologists, psychiatrists and nurses. Most have pointed out that those individuals who live with extreme passive behavioral styles are more likely to complain about being sick, tired, run down, possess nagging aches and pains, and suffer from depression. Passive individuals are most likely to be characterized as sponges and receptive canisters for other people's demands. They take in other people's garbage. It builds and builds until it overflows. These individuals feel like they are drowning in a toxic vat. These toxins poison them with thoughts of helplessness and depression. Some become so overwhelmed it incapacitates them.

Have you ever been around someone who projects a lot of negativity and despair? Do you enjoy listening to someone constantly complain about their circumstances? How does it make you feel? Well, if you possess compressive anger I am sure you feel like choking the hell out of them! Most people feel completely drained being around passive people. I refer to people such as these as "psychical vampires". They burden you and leave you feeling emotionally drained!

Most assertive people have a very low tolerance for passive people as they do aggressive people. You definitely get tired of carrying conversations, perhaps even relationships. Explosive types have next to zero tolerance for passives, as do passive-aggressive people. Interestingly, aggressive behavioral types thrive on passive people. They complete each others' utter dysfunction!

When you look at relationships where domestic violence exists, you can usually find one of the partners being the aggressive type while the other one is the passive type. In fact, you might view the aggressive individual and passive individual as one in the same but on different ends of the continuum.

AGGRESSIVE---PASSSIVE
(abuser/enforcer)   (victim/receiver)

Many passive individuals who are victims of abuse learned it from abusive and dysfunctional parents. They learned they needed to rely on others for nearly all facets of their lives. They were taught early on to become dependent on others. Hence, the term "co-dependency" arose from this type of dysfunctional relationship. I won't get into all the intricacies of how co-dependent relationships evolve, maintain and dissolve as you could read countless books and still get different opinions. There are good books on the subject. A couple of years ago I wrote a popular selling book *Why Women Want What They Can't Have* which explored the whole dynamics of relationships and abuse factors. I strongly recommend reading it if you have repeated failed relationships or are currently in a dysfunctional one. It will shed light on the "why's" and "what to do's".

Passive individuals definitely need to take assertiveness training workshops. The source of their problem is low self-esteem which leads to inferiority. When you build your self-esteem you become more self-sufficient and self-directed. This will definitely get you out of the doldrums of passivity and into the world of assertiveness if you practice it and stay with it.

Remember, this flowchart:

I THINK IT ---   >   I FEEL IT --- >   I ACT IT --- >   <u>I BECOME IT!</u>

Translated in positive and accountable terms:

I THINK ASSERTIVE THOUGHTS -- >FEEL ASSERTIVE --- >   ACT ASSERTIVE -→
<u>*I BECOME ASSERTIVE!*</u>

Hey, what do you have to lose?

17

HOW TO MANAGE YOUR ANGER!

☯

When angry count four; when very angry, swear.
Mark Twain

MANAGING YOUR ANGER

Everyone gets angry at some point. Anger is not a bad emotion, but it's how you act and use it which makes it detrimental! With that said, most people do a pretty good job at managing their emotions. On the other hand, there are those who don't and require new strategies for keeping their anger in check.

The anger management strategies I am about to discuss are geared toward those with anger management problems. These techniques were not created for individuals living with people with anger management problems. I do believe you can use them with angry people and it could de-escalate their anger. Keep in mind, this book was written for people dealing with anger management issues of their own who want to change!

I have been working with clients for nearly fifteen years. I have made suggestions for dealing with anger management based on what I have read in books, learned from other therapists and most importantly, from my clients. My clients are the best source of feedback for what works versus what needs to be modified. The most rewarding experience I have working with clients who have anger management problems is when they stop coming for counseling because their anger is in check. Whatever they did worked. They finally got it!

I often create anger management plans with clients offering them a variety of strategies. Most times, the client and myself decide what we think will work best for their personality and behavioral style.

Over the years, we have tried many methods for controlling and modifying detrimental anger. My clients use all of these approaches. I hope one or more work for you if you are having difficulty with managing your anger.

THE BIG ADIOS

I have been asked many times, is just walking away when you are angry a form of running away from your problems? My response is NO! Remember, you are the one with the anger management problem and depending on what kind of anger style you possess, you could do more harm than good if you choose to remain in your current situation.

The famous psychologist Dr. Albert Ellis wrote a book How Stop Others From Pushing Your Buttons. I think the book is exceptionally helpful and I used many of his principles when working with my own clients. Basically, it teaches you how to change your thinking patterns. If you are the explosive or aggressive type of individual who is put in situations where you don't have time to think things through immediately, sometimes "exit stage left" is going to be a better option for you. If your anger gets you into trouble with the law, your boss or with your family because you become violent, then this is perhaps your best option. It is better to have a job or family tomorrow and think things through rationally, than throw it all away in a New York minute!

      An important point I want to make is you shouldn't use this strategy for all situations all the time. If you do, then I would contend you are a runner. This strategy is a bandage solution until you get anger management counseling and support. Eventually, you will have to get to the root of what is making you angry. You can't run from everyone. Remember, conflict is good. It brings to the forefront the need for change. If you run whenever conflict or adversity stares you in the face, you will be the ultimate loser! You will miss out on opportunities for personal growth and positive change.

      Running is the best option when you run the risk of becoming violent or hurting someone. The people you are running from will probably be those who see you angry most of the time or push your buttons. Should they ask you where you are going, the best advice is to say nothing or that you'll talk to them later when you are calm. Let them know you are upset and then beat it! At this point if both of you haggle over who is going to get the last word in, then you will recreate the situation as it usually begins and ends, out of control!

Keep in mind, you are the one with the anger management problem. It is not your concern at that moment how the other person feels. It is important to recognize how you feel and get the hell out of there before ripping someone's head off!

LAMINATED REMINDERS

This strategy was suggested by a man who was charged with assaulting his girlfriend. My client has a very prominent position in society both with his career and the volunteer organizations he belongs too. One night he had too much to drink and proceeded to slap his girlfriend in public after he accused her of nagging him. He warned her to stop, but she wouldn't let up. He got the last word in with a slap and was charged with assault. He said this was the most embarrassing experience he had ever encountered as his name made page three of the local newspaper due to the incident. He was instructed by the judge to get anger management counseling and this is when he came to see me. We discussed what happened and how he was feeling after the incident. Fortunately for him, his girlfriend had forgiven him. All of the organizations he is involved with were also forgiving. He wanted to know what intervention he could put in place so an incident like this wouldn't happen again. After a couple of sessions, I learned from him that after he has a couple of drinks he becomes aggressive. I also learned that his greatest motivator is his fear of losing everything he had worked for. Up until that point he was driven by greed. He was greatly humbled by what happened. This incident was good in a way because it knocked him off his pedestal of greed. I think his fear of losing everything was a great new motivator. It encouraged him to change and shift away from greed as his primary motivator. It helped him realize that gain was a more acceptable motivating factor.

Together, we came up with the following game plan. First, he would have no more than one drink occasionally when out in public or with his girlfriend. I suggested he avoid drinking all together. His drinking was a by-product of his needing to unwind from his professional life. We discussed the "greed factors" he possessed and he agreed if he took his foot off the proverbial accelerator for success and put things on cruise control, then he wouldn't have to drink to take the edge off. He agreed to this and this helped a lot. In subsequent sessions we also discussed the reasons for his intense desire for success and learned he had self-esteem issues causing him to feel inferior. Months later when these revelations were unraveled and accepted, greed became non-existent.

In the initial duration, he needed something which would serve as a daily reminder for what had happened. He acknowledged the write-up in the local newspaper regarding his assault charge was very embarrassing. Just the sight of it made him sick. It literally made him want to vomit. Why not try the same principle they do with alcoholics using aversion therapy? Some alcoholics will use Antabuse, a drug which makes them violently ill whenever they drink. Well, I thought we would try "news clipping aversion therapy"!

I had him make several scaled down versions of the article and had him laminate them like credit cards. He was to carry one in his wallet, glove box of his car, brief case, etc. He was to always have one on hand. Also, if he went to the bar, he would take it out and place it next to his wallet as a reminder. This approach worked! It produced the results he wanted. He mentioned there were two near occasions for aggression and the card saved his bacon and got him out of the situation before it festered. Six years later, he is doing great and has learned to manage his anger!

    I realize everyone doesn't have a police report or newspaper clipping advertising their anger management issues. That is good thing! I do encourage individuals to try laminated reminder cards! For those clients who want to try this approach, I have them write down what they are afraid of on paper (in regards to their anger), something which makes them feel good (a loved one/child), or something spiritually motivating and have it laminated. For this to work, it has to be something which touches your heart and mind. It has to motivate you. It will stimulate your thinking process to the present moment. If it does, then it is a sure bet it will counteract your aggressive thought process. Give it a try, what do you have to lose? Don't be tomorrow's local news story!

PERSPECTIVE TAKING

In this approach, I teach clients what it feels like to be in another person's shoes. This approach is very much like assertiveness training. In assertiveness training, one of the key elements is reflective listening. I teach students who want to be counselors the skills for reflective listening. Most reflective listening training and skills come from the wonderful work of Carl Rogers and his Client-centered Therapy approach. I strongly recommend reading some of his books to master these skills.

Reflective listening skills are at the heart of perspective taking and can often de-escalate conflict and confrontations before they get out of hand. The two key ingredients for reflective listening are:

1) Listening with intention/active listening
2) Paraphrasing

Listening with intention requires listeners to become active participants in the conversation, not only in speaking but also in listening. When most people communicate, they think of what they are going to say or how they will answer while the other person is talking. Rather than fully devoting their undivided attention to the speaker, they are contemplating possible responses.

Listening with intention involves just what it implies. You listen to both the denotation and connotation of the speech. Denotation is the superficial surface level dialogue others offer us when they speak. Denotation is the simple spoken word. The gist of what is said. Connotation on the other hand is the emotional, subjective meaning underlying the words. Connotation provides the ingredients which gives words true meaning. Always remember, words don't mean, people do!

To listen with intention means to listen for the true meaning within spoken words. Rather than analyzing the words themselves, active listening requires the listener to seek out the true intention for what was said. When you focus on the intention of words spoken, your mind no longer has time to dwell on confrontational and aggressive responses. If you are a hot-head always waiting for the chance to respond to further fuel the argument, this approach might save headache and regret.

Sometimes people say things they don't mean or say

things in the heat of the moment without thinking first. Their subjectivity over-rides their objectivity. Many prolonged arguments and fall-outs are the result of misspoken or unintended words. If you are the type of individual who possesses conflictual anger, then situations such as these are prime catalysts for your ire! Remember, you are the one with the anger management problem and it is not the other person's fault for getting you all bent out of shape and "making" you aggressive. You are in control of your mind and body. How you decide to respond is up to you. Remember, no one can make you angry! That decision is totally up to you. My guess is, if you have a personality which thrives on conflict and manipulation, then you are probably chomping at the bit to fire counter-attacks during arguments. In fact, you are most likely an individual who likes to strike below the belt or launch stored up grievances at the other person. Listening with intention helps to deviate from your conflictual, aggressive thought process. When you are too busy listening with intention, you are distracting yourself from your own irrational thought process, you're need to argue.

What would you think if I said, "its raining cats and dogs"? If you listen without intention, then you are just listening to the spoken words. You probably say to yourself, "so what, big frigging deal!" On the other hand, when you listen with intention to, "it's raining cats and dogs", you might see I have offered you something a little more profound than just the basic spoken words. I might have actually uttered this statement because I care about you, it's cold and rainy, and I don't want you to catch a cold. Argumentative people usually pay attention to the superficial part of this statement and get ready to say something sarcastic in return. "What do you think, I am an idiot and blind that I can't see that it is raining?" You may even take the implication the other person is insulting you and asserting you are incapable of taking care of yourself. On the other hand, the subjective meaning implies the other person really cares about you and your well-being. Funny, sometimes we disagree over something we are in total agreement over due to the interpretation and intention of the remarks people make.

Paraphrasing is the process of seeking clarification or reaffirming what the other person has said. Paraphrasing is putting into your own words what the other person has said to you. It clarifies to you and the speaker the true intention and meaning for what has been said. This alone can prevent misunderstandings and ugly arguments. Clarification is important as it guards against the word ASSUME. I am sure you know what assume stands for:

ASS / U / ME

You don't want to make an ass of yourself or the other person! Reaffirming allows the listener to stick too or alter their point of reference. If you agree with what the speaker has said, then you can attest to what they are saying. On the other hand, should you disagree, then you can protest what is being said. Either way it lets the speaker know you are listening to them instead of firing off responses created before hand.

If you go back to my original example, "it's raining "cats and dogs", paraphrasing would clarify and reaffirm the spoken meaning and the intention of this statement. For example:

ORIGINAL STATEMENT: *It's raining cats and dogs.*

PARAPHRASE: *It sounds to me like it's really raining hard.*

CLARIFICATION: *If I hear you correctly, you are concerned* *for my well being and you don't want me to get wet.*

The individual you are having this discussion with can now respond back to you in either agreement or disagreement.

The major goal of perspective taking is to keep the lines of communication open. If you possess aggression, practicing this approach shows others you are open-minded and willing to listen. If you were to continue to practice your rigid thinking process and be less responsive to listening to others, you will soon get the label "stubborn" or "hardhead". People will not want to talk to you because they know all you want to do is argue. They will perceive you as not wanting to listen to them because what they have to say is less important. I cannot reiterate this point enough! Perspective taking gets you out of your combative attitude as it obstructs your argumentativeness and encourages listening. If you want to see the quality of your relationships and social interactions improve, I strongly recommend using this approach!

OWN YOUR FEELINGS!

Whenever I work with clients one on one, or in anger

management groups, one of the first points I present to them is that no one person can make you angry unless you allow yourself to become angry. Not surprisingly, clients strongly object to my "ridiculous" statement. I usually smile at them and ask them if they think I could make them do something against their will. I've even gone so far as to ask, "Could I be your God or better yet, some perverse puppeteer who can make you do whatever I want, even making you angry?" Of course they think about it for a moment. Before they are ready to offer me an answer, I badger them with another quick question, "Do you think your wife, husband, boss, or whomever makes you mad is God over your life?" They usually offer me a very definitive "No"! I then have them stop in their tracks and ask them to rethink what they were just trying to convince me of. Here is the line of reasoning I provide them with:

"Okay, it is your spouse, or boss who makes you angry, right? Well, if they can make you angry, then I am sure they are responsible for all of your other emotions as well, joy, sadness, fear, etc. Right? Just think about what you are telling me! Furthermore, think about what you are trying to convince yourself of. You are leading yourself to believe others are

responsible for what you are feeling or not feeling. You are basically an empty emotional mind waiting to be fed and filled by others. Also, once filled, you become a puppet. They can then make you dance around however way they choose. You are pretty much like a monkey dancing around to the sounds of the organ the puppeteer is grinding. Poor you! Sounds like you can't make any emotional decisions for yourself. Someone literally has their hand stuck in your backside and you are their dummy sitting on their knee! They truly are God to you. How does that make you feel?"

At this point, there is usually a prolonged moment of silence as my clients ponder what I have just said. The silence is usually broken by a nervous laugh, snorting, head-shaking or knee slapping. The response I hear next is one I'd swear was memorized by each client, "Wow, I never thought of it that way!" Once more, there is usually a prolonged silence as my clients ponder this new revelation. Almost like clockwork the next comment or question they make is always the same, "It's only my wife who gets under my skin." "It's only my husband who annoys the hell out of me!" "My kids are on my last nerve." "I hate my boss and my place of work!"

If you go back to the beginning of this book, I asked you to make a list of the people, situations or things which you get most angry at. I am sure the same person or situation heads your list in frequency. It's not like they were purposely put on this planet to annoy you even though you might want to believe that! Rather, you have created an "anger script" in your mind toward this person whereby you make them the villain or source of your angst. You give them power they don't possess. Even if they did have some power over you, it is how you choose to respond which determines their degree of mastery over you. I want you to remember the following:

> 1) You own your feelings and only you can feel your emotions.
> 2) No one can control you unless you let them.
> 3) Even when you let someone control you, you are still in total control as you choose how you will allow them to manipulate you.
> 4) Accusing others for making you mad or creating other emotions in you allows you to try to escape responsibility for what you are thinking and feeling.

5) No one including yourself can make you feel angry unless you first think something to stimulate your emotions.

6) Only you can decide on whether to get angry or not, just as you can decide to get sexually aroused or not. Contrary to popular opinion, what gets aroused below the waist can only get excited once the brain perceives excitement and arousal! The same holds true for anger.

7) The mind can only devote its full attention to one thing at a time! If someone around you is trying to engage you in a conflict and you are too busy fantasizing about some tropical oasis, the likelihood of you getting upset isn't very high!

8) Those you get angry with the most are usually people close to you who you have an emotional vested interest in.

9) Perhaps the reason you are really getting mad is you wish to be the puppeteer (controlling) and others are not co-operating with you!

10) Why should everything always have to go your way or be the way you like it? Perhaps

you are a perfectionist putting too much pressure on yourself and others!

In perspective taking I discussed active listening while engaging others in conversation. Guess what? When you own your feelings, you actively listen to your thought process! What are you telling yourself to make yourself angry? There must be something. Others can't annoy you unless you perceive them as an annoyance and you make yourself upset at the thought of them. Perhaps you have a stereotypical mental script for each person you deal with in your daily life. Situations always turn out the same because your thoughts, actions and behaviors are scripted based on previous encounters. Moreover, if you are using repetitious scripts with the same individuals, they are probably doing the same with you as they have told themselves, "Here we go again!" We are very much like Pavlov's dogs. Over a period of time we respond the same way to the same individuals because we perceive them as remaining in a flux state (stimulus) and we respond the same way without applying any active thought process (response).

WHAT'S YOUR ANGER TYPE?

When you and your spouse argue or fight all the time I'll bet it looks like the same movie playing itself over and over again. Do you see the same cast of characters? Do you also see the same scene or plot? At the rate you're disputes are going, they're probably close to catching up to the cheesy slasher movie sequels! If one or both of you start wearing goalie masks, then I would definitely start to worry!

I want you to go back to the example of the organ grinder and the monkey. I want you to picture it in your mind. Who actually controls who? Does the monkey dance because the organ grinder plays the music? Are people amused by the monkey jumping around? Or does the monkey dance to make the organ grinder play more music in order to make him look silly and ridiculous in his costume? Who looks silly? In constant domestic disputes, there is always an organ grinder and a monkey. Which one are you? If you choose to own your emotions, no one can control you. In fact, you start to gain better control over your own thought process. You no longer become a circus side show, rather a very polished performer! The choice to think, feel, act and become is always yours.

STAY IN THE PRESENT

Most people get a great sense of comfort from reliving emotions and experiences from the past. Interestingly, the emotions and experiences are not always pleasant ones! Some people prefer to hold onto negative experiences because it gives them a sense of perceived power or comfort. As discussed earlier, this is at the root of petrified anger!

Why do so many people choose to live in the past? The answer is quite simple. They derive a sense of comfort from the past because it is non-threatening. They already know what has happened. The future has yet to come so we have no control over the future. The same can be said about the past. We have no control over the past because it has already happened. We cannot go back and change it!

The only time frame we possess total control over is the present. What I find most interesting when I work with clients is they resist feeling and existing in the present the most! The reason why is they have to invest thought and emotion into the present and for some, this is quite threatening! Furthermore, to work in the present means to change existing negative thought patterns. This takes a lot of work and some people are not willing to invest the time, energy or emotions. They hold onto what they know even though it is detrimental and negative, rather than risk gaining something more positive. Generally speaking, when it comes to self-analysis and change, most people are lazy!

If you are an individual possessing an anger management problem which is habitual and petrified, you need to get out of the past! If time traveling machines in movies really existed, then life truly would be so much easier. You could go back and change things. Unfortunately, these movies are fantastical. Your anger management problem is real and requires change!

In essence, you have to create your own mental time traveling machine which will keep your emotions in the present state. This is paramount when you are involved with people you perceive as having wronged you in the past. I am sure you are able to transport yourself back in time in a blink of an eye to the unfortunate situation you were a part of involving the other person. This gets the juices flowing, the pulse racing and the angry thoughts recurring all over again. You need to stop this if you are ever going to move on!

There are several questions I ask clients to think about

when discussing their anger:

1) How is getting angry today undoing what happened in the past?
2) How is getting angry now making you feel good in the present?
3) Can you actually go back and change what happened?
4) Do you think those who did wrong to you still dwell on what happened and get as upset as you?
5) Do you believe you are in control of yourself right here, right now in the present?
6) If you answered yes to the last question, what do you want to feel right now? What would make you feel great?
7) If vengeance or ill harm is wished upon the person from the past, then you are not living in the present! How can you get into a positive, present feeling state now? What is a positive, happy thought for you now?
8) What goals would you like to set for yourself

which will make you a "present moment" thinker?

👍

I like to spend at least one session going through this process to allow clients to recognize a few things:

1) You can only control the present.
2) Only you control your thoughts, feelings and actions.
3) The past will always remain unchanged.
4) Your present will soon become the past and wouldn't you rather build on healthier pasts?
5) Anything you choose to be or do is up to you.

👍

This exercise teaches clients autonomy, empowerment and hope. They are taught to teach themselves daily, hourly, or moment to moment reminders to live in the present. Once you do this enough times, living in the present becomes second nature. In fact, you become so into living in the present it distracts your thought processes from drifting back into the past. You can't think of past wrongs done to you when you are thinking about feeling good right now!

PARROTING

Parroting is a bizarre yet interesting approach which works well for individuals with compressive anger who like yelling. Interestingly, I learned this approach by watching children get their way with parents. It is a tenacious, "wear them out" approach which usually does get results!

When you were a child did you ever drive your parents insane during long car rides asking repeatedly, "Are we there yet?" Do you remember how crazy this use to make your parents? They were willing to do just about anything to shut you up! Being a nag actually does have it's virtues on occasion.

What is important to remember is you possess the anger management problem and you will try using this approach to prevent yourself from blowing up and screaming at those who push your buttons. Furthermore, if you're nagging bothers them, then it becomes their issue to contend with. I am only suggesting what might work at de-escalating your compressive anger. Rather than you exploding, you will get to be the nag and drive someone else nuts for a change!

Parroting works just as it suggests. You repeat the same thing over and over again until you get what you want. You are not hurting, harming or threatening anyone. In fact, you are basically asserting your intention on the other person and leaving it up to them to respond.

This approach works remarkably well if you are a parent having difficulty getting your kids to listen to you. I have taught this approach to several clients. They have used it with their children tweaking it here and there. In the end, it usually produces favorable results. Kids start doing what they are asked to do so their parents will stop nagging them.

A great success story for this technique involved a gentleman I had as a client a few years ago. He was married to a woman who had a teenage son from a previous marriage. The son did not like him and often would start arguments between his parents. My client had an anger management problem which was deeply embedded in compressive anger. He claimed he could go from zero to sixty in under a second. He would erupt on his stepson whenever he didn't do what he was told.

He would leave the fourteen year old chores to complete while he was at work. The teenager would never do what he was told due to laziness and defiance. This would set my client off when he came home from work. Things would escalate into a war between he and his wife. One night he actually grabbed the teen and shook him around. His wife threatened to leave him if an event like this ever happened again. My client came to me looking for ways to control his anger when his stepson defied him.

    I explained the parroting method to him and he thought I was nuts! I asked him what did he have to lose except his marriage? He agreed to try it. He was instructed to remain calm next time a chore was not completed. He was to approach the son and sit next to him and politely point out what he didn't do. If he still didn't complete the chore, he was to follow him around all day and night, nicely bringing it to his attention. He used little post-it reminders all over the house. My client found humor in this and actually thought it would be fun to try. He viewed it as a perverse form of psychological punishment toward the teen. He loved it! He tried it and guess what? It worked!

    He reported his wife was not too impressed with the

approach but if it prevented him from losing it, then she would co-operate since it was her ultimatum that he receive anger management. He decided to modify it and took it one step further. He actually called the son's school to speak with the principle. The principle called the boy to the office and gave him his stepfather's message, "The lawn needs to be cut!" He was so embarrassed by the message and the worry of him doing it again that the first thing he did when he went home was cut the lawn. My client couldn't get him to complete this chore for more than three weeks and just like that, the lawn was cut weekly without further grief. I should also add, my client's wife is now using this same approach with my client. What goes around indeed comes around!

CATHARTIC SUBLIMATION

Catharsis means to release or relieve stress. Sublimation means to direct your aggression onto socially acceptable activities. Sublimation comes from Psychoanalysis. It is a defense mechanism used to direct unacceptable sexual feelings or aggression onto something society views as acceptable. For example, instead of punching your spouse or kicking the cat, you go and strike a punching bag. Cathartic sublimation is great for those possessing lots of stress and frustration who need a safe target to direct it at. This approach is highly recommended to all even if you do not have anger management problems. It is a great method for stress reduction.

Most people are weighed down by the burdens of everyday living. They are highly stressed and seek some kind of escape. I recommend this technique if you have lots of stress in your life, or if you are just seeking some sort of escape. Here is a list of some of the activities my clients swear by:

- working out/exercise
- walking/hiking
- meditating
- martial arts
- comedy (television/movies)
- swimming
- gardening
- listening to music
- shopping
- weekend getaways/vacations

WHAT'S YOUR ANGER TYPE?

- long drives
- reading
- painting
- playing with pets
- praying
- napping

👍

Since everyone is different, it is best to select a cathartic activity you find most relaxing and non-taxing. Just taking a 15 to 20 minute walk each day will do wonders for calming your mind and body. Also, if you are cooped up in doors all the time, I highly recommend getting outside and enjoying fresh air and nature. The key aspect of this exercise is to remove yourself as far away as possible from the rigors of everyday living. You might call this a brief vacation from reality. Give it a try, it may work wonders for you!

DEFLECTING

Deflecting is one of the more interesting techniques developed for people with severe anger problems. It also works very well for those who have a hard time taking criticism. Don't get me wrong, criticism is a good thing. When given constructively and taken constructively, you can really work on improving yourself. Unfortunately, when criticism is tossed out during arguments, it is rarely given constructively or taken constructively!

Deflecting is a technique which is not for the squeamish! It requires the individual with the anger management problem to remain cool, calm and composed for it to work. You are probably saying to yourself that if you possessed these attributes in the first place, you wouldn't need this technique or this book! Yes, you're right, but this technique is great for recreating the dynamics in relationships with those you have detrimental conflict and anger issues with. It really does work if you will exercise patience and practice!

Earlier I discussed how many relationships possessing conflict and dysfunction operate like a movie replaying itself repetitiously. Those involved along with yourself are like actors playing the same roles over and over again. You have created solidified cognitive scripts which you play out to the tee. The argument begins the same way, plays out the same way and ends the same way, or sometimes harsher. This is not good! You have become sensitized to the script and have become a lazy thinker. You have chosen to remain the same in your perceptions and responses to the other person. This buttresses the person's perception of you, who you are in conflict with. This enables their "lazy" script to be acted out yet again! What you have developed is a Pavlovian stimulus-response situation. I am sure it is difficult to determine who is figuratively ringing whose bell in your situation because it has grown so old!

Perhaps the greatest instigator of personal insult is name-calling. No one likes to be called names. If someone makes fun of your appearance, weight, flaws, defects, you take it to heart. It hurts like hell! Your response is typical, you come out swinging! The worst is when someone hits you below the belt with their comments which rip through your weak spots whatever they may be. Ever notice as an argument becomes more personal with someone close, you start to throw everything you can muster at that person? You literally chuck everything at them accept the kitchen sink. Thank God that's bolted down or that too would probably be flying!

When you get into heated discussions with people you are closest with, family and friends, it seems they have a way of yanking onto your greatest heart strings. I am sure most don't try to intentionally hurt you, but their emotions get the better of them during heated arguments. All rationale and objectivity is thrown out the window when the gloves come off. Since they are so close to you, they know how to hit you below the belt using past transgressions. Even though some people claim to have forgiven you for what you did in the past, it appears they haven't truly forgotten during arguments. They nail you with what bothers you the most. It's as if they have stored up grievances to be used against you during arguments. They know your vulnerabilities!

If you are the individual who erupts when someone starts attacking you, then deflecting may be your best line of defense. In fact, it may be the best and only anger management technique you may ever need to use. Remember, this approach is used by individuals with anger management problems when dealing with others who definitely know how to provoke them. It is a great approach for modifying "lazy" argumentative scripts for both of you. If you change your script, then the other person will have to change their own because it no longer produces the same results or ignites the same response. Fasten your seatbelts and learn how it works!

Firstly, you will need to re-train your own thinking process. Tell yourself that individuals who verbally attack you are insecure and desperate. This is the honest truth. If someone has to try and put you down to make themselves feel more superior, it is because they have low self-esteem, plain and simple! Once you give in to put downs, you help increase their perceived superiority over you. Don't fall into this trap! Try to view the individual attacking you as emotionally delayed in their social skills. Perceive them as a little child requiring attention. Face it, if a child calls you names you are less likely to take it to heart because you make note of where it is coming from. Do the same with adults who try to put you down. Once you perceive them as a child in an adult's body, thank them for whatever they are telling you, or pleasantly agree with them.

I am sure you are probably thinking I am nuts for suggesting this. Trust me, it really does work! The following is a great instance from a client I worked with whose wife was emotionally and mentally abusive toward him. After being goaded into arguments, he could not handle the mental abuse and would literally/figuratively come out swinging. He was growing more physically abusive each time. The couple really did love each other, neither of them wanting a divorce. It really was a case of "can't live with them, can't live without them!" Since he came to me for anger management, I offered this technique to him. He commented I was crazy for even suggesting this approach. He refused to try it. I suggested he get a good lawyer since the next physical attack on his wife may get him arrested, or even kill her! Even though he kept claiming it was all his wife's fault for calling him names, I informed him he had the ultimate control over his emotions and actions. By controlling himself and choosing to change his responses, he would inadvertently motivate her to change. In fact, both would realize she could no longer "control" the situation as he put it. He agreed to try it. The key attributes required when using this approach are perseverance and persistence. There is no going back once you start it or else it reaffirms the other person's belief that they can provoke you at will!

Here was what this client claimed his wife was doing which would send him over the edge:

WHAT'S YOUR ANGER TYPE?

"My wife calls me names all the time. She is a fitness fanatic, and I am not. As you can see I am very much overweight. She calls me a fat pig! She calls me various dinosaur-related names. She tells me I'm disgusting. She says I am a terrible lover. She makes fun of my manhood! She makes negative comments about my family. I recently got laid off and she says I am totally useless. I am trying to find new work or upgrade my schooling. She accuses me of being a loser. Funny part is she says she hates me when we fight, but after she will apologize and still say it's my fault. I really do love her and she says she loves me! I really do feel bad whenever I shove her or hit her."

How would deflecting work in this situation? How could it help change this detrimental and abusive condition? Deflecting taught my client the following:

1) Perceive your wife as a big kid who feels insecure at times, especially when she makes derogatory comments to you.

2) You are to take each insult and turn them around into

perceived constructive criticisms. You will thank her for pointing out your short-comings.

For example: *"You are a fat pig!"*
Your response*: "Thank you honey for pointing out I have a weight problem. I am glad you are concerned for my well-being."*

3) You are to act and appear sincere when responding to insults. Avoid showing displeasure or anger. When someone senses this, they smell blood in the water!

4) When the next round of attacks happen as I am sure they will, offer a short smile with a kind, agreeable statement.

For example: *"Gee honey, you've really pointed out some things I need to work on. I love you for that."*

5) If and when you feel your blood and ire boiling, remain calm and walk away offering a gratuitous statement.

For example: *"Sweetheart, you've given me lots to think about and I will go and do some thinking right now. Thank you."*

6) Get out of there! I am sure parting shots will be fired your way. Whenever this happens, say nothing or tell the person you care.

For example: *"I love you too."*

7) Always remember, you are the one with the aggression or compressive anger problem. You can't afford to lose it and hit the other person!

8) As you use this technique more and become more comfortable with it, use mild humor and smile whenever someone rips into you. It shows the other person, at least outwardly you are not bothered by put downs.

Remember way back when in elementary school how teachers used to tell students to ignore the class clown? By ignoring the class clown, they would realize no one was stimulated by their antics and they would be forced to move onto something more stimulating, hopefully schoolwork! The same is true in relationship disputes. The other person will realize your triggers can no longer be manipulated and they will have to find more mature means for capturing and holding your attention!

    The client who I used as an example used this technique to perfection and it really did change the dynamics of his marriage and saved it! His wife was forced to modify her own behaviors. They now have 2 children and everything is much better. This is not to say they don't argue anymore. It is how they argue which is now making the difference!

    If all else fails, then I would suggest trying this approach. It does take practice and patience on your part. You have to work it through and over time I believe you will get the positive results my clients have gotten. Happy deflecting!

18

CHILDREN AND ANGER

☺

Anybody can become angry - that is easy; but to be angry with the right person, and to the right degree, and at the right time, and for the right purpose, and in the right way - that is not within everybody's power and is not easy.

Aristotle

WHAT'S YOUR ANGER TYPE?

One of the growing complaints I keep hearing from parents and teachers today is how angry children are becoming! As a professor, I am constantly informed of the plethora of workshops and organizations focusing on childhood bullying. Why is there so much aggression and bullying going on in children and teens? Colleagues of mine and parents I have spoken with have a number of their own hypotheses.

Some believe it is due to the high incidence of attention deficit and hyperactivity disorders, along with other mental health disorders children possess. Others assert it is due to the media. Kids are watching more television shows and movies which promote sex and aggression. The most popular types of video and Internet games kids are playing are usually laden with violence. Furthermore, I have heard parents argue it is because of incompetent teachers and poor educational systems. On the other hand, I have heard several teachers assert it is due to insufficient parenting skills and discipline. Take your pick!

What do I think is the cause of higher incidences of anger in children? For starters, I believe there is a combination of factors. I would cite some of the reasons just mentioned. Having worked with families, couples and children in therapy, I do believe the ultimate cause of angry children is rooted in dysfunctional families. From what I have experienced, three distinct precipitating factors stand out:

> 1) Communication within the family circle is non-existent or minimal at best.
>
> 2) One or both parents, as well as older siblings and extended family members use aggression regularly in their daily lives and this is witnessed by younger children.
>
> 3) Children are being verbally, emotionally, physically or sexually abused.

Anger very much follows a simple physics principle for matter: You can't get something from nothing! Anger in children had to be born from something. Kids either had to experience it first hand (victim) or witness it. Family dynamics precipitate emotions and perhaps external stimuli such as media or peers serve as catalysts.

Let's examine each of the three factors I suggested:

LACK OF COMMUNICATION

In other books and articles I have written, I often use statistics I have heard or learned from professionals and experts specializing in communication. One statistic I heard is very much worth noting in this chapter. According to some experts, did you know the average amount of time parents engage in effective and productive communication with their children is under 10 minutes per day? Every time I hear statistics like this I am floored! Is it any wonder children lack self-discipline skills? Furthermore, do you think some children feel neglected enough to use anger as a means for getting attention?

For parents who believe I am way off base, then I would welcome feedback from you telling me what you think the reason is. If your kids are messed up because of society and media, then why haven't you intervened? If it's due to bad teachers and school systems, then why not put your kids in private schools or boot camps? I have found the best parents are those who recognize they are both part of the problem and part of the solution when they have kids with anger management problems. Furthermore, those who keep passing the buck and believing it's everyone else's fault are living in a fantasy world. Interestingly, to admit your child has an anger problem might lead you to admit you have one yourself! If you choose to just keep sweeping the dirt under the rug, there won't be a shovel big enough to scoop up the crap that will eventually grow to knee deep!

If you engage your children in active communication on a daily basis, you will know what your kids are thinking and feeling. Help to shape their lives instead of shipping them out to someone else to do what you should be doing. Love your children instead of neglecting their emotional needs. Neglect fuels anger because children get tired of feeling abandoned and unwanted.

WITNESSING AGGRESSION IN THE HOME

How can anyone witnessing aggression and dysfunction on a regular basis not be affected by it? Children who grow up in homes where anger is a staple emotion expect it. They start to view it as the norm for thinking, feeling, behaving and acting. Albert Bandura's Social Learning Theory is very accurate in aggressive, dysfunctional homes. Children observe aggressive behavior from those they model or emulate. Over a period of time they learn aggression works for getting what you want. Monkey see, monkey do! If you act like a barbaric ape, your child is most likely to become like you. Remember, you taught them to swing from the tree! For as long as I have been a therapist, I have never counseled a client who came from an extreme dysfunctional family who didn't possess some kind of depression, anxiety or personality disorder. Frankly, personality disorders are not good!

    Parents can help facilitate positive personality growth in their children if they recognize their own dysfunction. In working through your own anger and aggression problems you are applying preventative medicine for your own children in becoming the next generation of aggressors. If and when you are told by others to get family counseling, anger management or some kind of social support to remedy family dynamics, I strongly advise you take this input as constructive, helpful criticism. Moreover, when you see your child acting out and getting into trouble, this is a sign that an intervention is needed. Things need to change before they worsen and rankle out of control. Preventative medicine is the best approach!

BEING A VICTIM

I mentioned I never worked with a client who witnessed dysfunction on a regular basis and developed a healthy psyche. Most people who are victims of abuse grow tired of it and will eventually come out swinging. I have heard from experts asserting that children who are abused at home usually take it out on other children or teachers at school. Conversely, children who are bullied at school are more likely to abuse younger, smaller siblings, even their parents. Being abused and constantly witnessing violence creates cold, hostile aggressive feelings. At some point, people reach their maximum boiling point and snap! Has your child received too much abuse that they have reached their boiling point? Who will they take their aggression out on? Perhaps it might be you!

When you are fed something long enough, you eventually become it. Remember the old expression, you are what you eat! You get fed enough vile and violence and you will definitely become it since you know it best! Parents perpetuate violence in their own children by constantly abusing them. Abuse is wrong! If you are abusing your children, stop! You are creating the next chip off the old block, perhaps worse!

Teach your children abuse and violence is not the answer. You can undo what has been done if you recognize it sooner instead of later. Remember, your kids look up to you. You are their primary role model. You need to set the example for them to live by.

    I chatted with Dr. Bernie Seigel, the famous medical doctor best known for his work with children and patients suffering from terminal illness. Bernie as he is known by his beloved readers and fans truly believes in the healing of the soul and the promotion of love. He especially promotes this concept in parent-child relationships. He believes parents should always persist in loving their children which teaches them loving behavior. If you are loving your kids, you are not teaching them anger and hatred!

    There are many great books focusing on children and behavioral/anger management problems. My expertise is adults. I have included a suggested reading list of some good books in the appendices which I highly recommend.

19

TIRED OF FIGHTING?

The world needs anger. The world often continues to allow evil because it isn't angry enough.
               Bede Jarrett

WHAT'S YOUR ANGER TYPE?

Anger is a normal healthy emotion. Always remember, it is how you use it which makes it productive and helpful, or destructive and detrimental. To be angry is to celebrate your humanity. You have the right to think, feel and act. No one should ever tell you not to get angry. That is your right. In fact, more people should get angry. Perhaps this will initiate the changes which are needed in today's society!

Anger is a sign that something is discomforting and change is needed. Most people are afraid of change and avoid it like the plague. Interestingly, most would rather get angry and bitch about the way things are, rather than get angry and try to make a difference. Anger signifies dissatisfaction and a call for action. Use your anger assertively, productively and with good intention. When you use your anger with positive intention, you will strive toward win-win situations!

The purpose of this book was to help readers with anger management problems realize they can control their anger and that it need not control them. The key points I want readers to take with them can be summarized in 10 short thoughts:

1) You always own your emotions.
2) No one can make you mad.

3) Anger like any emotion will not last forever.

4) You need to identify triggers for your anger.

5) Life is too short to stay mad at someone.

6) Just as there are differences in people, there are differences in types of anger.

7) Find the anger management technique which works best for you.

8) Seeking arguments will most likely always initiate anger.

9) Never go to bed angry.

10) You can feel whatever you choose to feel.

ANGER INVENTORY

Now that you've finished reading this book, you can apply the principles and strategies to your own life. I suggest reading this book through again, especially the chapters which pertain to you. Over the next 30 days, keep a log of events, situations or instances when you feel angry. Fill out the following form. I recommend duplicating this form so you have several copies for each day in which you do these exercises.

1) What types of anger do I possess?

2) In which situations/people I am with, in or around did my anger get precipitated?

3) On a scale of 1-10, how did I handle my anger today?

4) Very important! What was I telling myself or thinking about at the time I got angry? What was my self-talk which made me made? Take 5-10 minutes to relive this situation and meditate on it.

5) What could I have done differently instead of getting angry? What can I do next time a similar situation arises? What thoughts do I need to retrain?

6) What anger management strategies will work best for me? Which one should I learn/practice?

7) Is there an anger management support group within my community I can join should my anger problems get worse? It is always good to have a safety valve!

8) Is there an "anger management buddy" I can find to vent with whenever extreme situations arise? Perhaps visiting a therapist for counseling might help.

9) Parting thoughts… You choose to be angry or you can choose not to be angry!

APPENDICES

REFERENCE SOURCES

MOVIES

Raging Bull
1980 Directed by Martin Scorsese

Single White Female
1992 Directed by Barbet Schroeder

The Talented Mr. Ripley
1999 Directed by Anthony Minghella

BOOKS

The Individual Psychology of Alfred Adler: A Systematic Presentation in Selections from His Writings. (1967). Heinz L. Ansbacher, editor & Rowena R. Ansbacher, editor. Publisher: Harper & Row. Place of Publication: New York.

Albert Bandura (1977). ***Social Learning Theory***, Prentice-Hall, Englewood Cliffs, N.J.

Eric Berne (1964). ***Games People Play : The basic handbook of transactional analysis.***

Margaret J. Black and Stephen A. Mitchell, (1995). ***Freud and Beyond: A History of Modern Psychoanalytic Thought.*** Basic Books. Place of Publication: New York.

Walter B. Cannon (1939). ***The Wisdom of the Body.*** Second edition, W. W. Norton, New York.

Dale Carnegie (1936). ***How to Win Friends & Influence People.*** Simon and Schuster Inc.

David P. Celani (1994). ***The Illusion of Love: Why the Battered Woman Returns to Her Abuser.*** Columbia University Press.

Compact American Medical Dictionary: A concise and Up-To-Date Guide To Medical Terms. American Heritage Dictionaries.

Diagnostic and Statistical Manual of Mental Disorders - Fourth Edition (DSM-IV), published by the American Psychiatric Association, Washington D.C., 1994, the main diagnostic reference of Mental Health professionals in the United States of America.

Albert Ellis and Arthur Lange, (1995). ***How To Keep People From Pushing Your Buttons.*** Citadel Press.

Edward Hoffman, (1996). ***The Drive for Self: Alfred Adler and the Founding of Individual Psychology.*** Addison Wesley (Current Publisher: Perseus Publishing). Place of Publication: Reading, MA.

Dario Nardi, (2001). ***Multiple Intelligences and Personality Type: Multiple Intelligences and Personality Type.***
I.P. Pavlov, (1925). ***"Twenty years of objective study of the higher nervous activity (behaviour) of animals."*** State publication, 3rd edition. Articles, Nos. 1, 2, 3, 4, 7, B, 10, 11, 13, 17, 20, 21, 23, 28, 29, 31, 33, 35.

Don Richard Riso and Russ Hudson, (2003). ***Discovering Your Personality Type: The Essential Introduction to the Enneagram.***

C.R. Rogers and R. Sanford, (1984). Client-centered psychotherapy. In Kaplan, H. and Sadock, B. (Eds.). ***Comprehensive textbook of Psychiatry/IV.*** pp. 1374-1388. Baltimore: Williams & Wilkins.

C.R. Rogers and B. Stevens, (1968). ***Person to person: The problem of being human.*** Lafayette, CA: Real People Press.

C.R. Rogers, (1951). ***Client-centered therapy: Its current practice, implications and theory.*** Boston: Houghton Mifflin.

H. Selye, (1956). ***The Stresses Of Life.*** McGraw Hill.

H. Selye, (1955). ***Stress And Disease.*** Science 1955; 122:625.

H. Selye, (1952). ***The Story of the Adaptation Syndrome.*** Montreal, Quebec, Canada: Acta Inc. Med. Pub.

Bartlett H. Stoodley, (1959). ***The Concepts of Sigmund Freud.*** Free Press. Place of Publication: Glencoe, IL.

RECOMMENDED READINGS

The Success Principles
Jack Canfield, and Janet Switzer

Defining Mental Health As A Public Health Problem
William Glasser M.D.

Cracking The Millionaire Code
Mark Victor Hansen and Robert G. Allen

Don't Throw Away Tomorrow
Robert H. Schuller.

Meditations For Overcoming Life's Stresses And Strains
Bernie Siegel M.D.

Not to People Like Us: The Hidden Abuse in Upscale Marriages
Dr. Susan Weitzman

CHILDREN AND ANGER

Defying the Defiance
Tip Frank, Mike Paget & Jerry Wilde

Adult Children: The Secrets of Dysfunctional Families
John Friel

Healthy Anger: How to Help Children and Teens Manage Their Anger
Bernard Golden

Parenting the Explosive Child: the Collaborative Problem Solving Approac
Ross Greene & Stuart Ablon,

The Explosive Child: a New Approach for Understanding and Parenting Easily Frustrated, Chronically Inflexible Children
Ross Greene

Seeing Red: an Anger Management and Peacemaking Curriculum for Kid
Jennifer Simmonds

The Parent's Book About Bullying: Changing the Course of Your Child's Life
William Voors

Treating Troubled Children and Their Families
Ellen F. Wachtel

www.parentbooks.ca

ABOUT PETER ANDREW SACCO

Peter has been working with individuals in private practice and support groups for over a decade. Peter specializes in anger management classes, workshops/seminars, individual coaching and counseling. As a professor, he teaches at universities and colleges both in the United States and Canada. He teaches courses in addiction studies, police studies, criminal psychology and education. Peter continues to produce television shows and was the host of "Mental Health Matters".

Peter continues to write articles for magazines, as well as serving as Editor-in-Chief for Vices: The Magazine For Addictions And Habits. Other books Peter has written include:

WHY WOMEN WANT WHAT THEY CAN'T HAVE

FEAR FACTORS.

To learn more about Peter and his work or to book him for a speaking engagement, please visit his website: www.petersacco.com

Printed in the United States
113064LV00001B/134/A